By the Same Author

Stand-Up Comedy: The Book

THE
HOMO
HANDBOOK

Getting in Touch with Your Inner Homo

JUDY CARTER

FIRESIDE BOOKS

In memory of my grandmother,
LEAH SILVERMAN,
who gave me a lot of love
and a lot of laughs

FIRESIDE
Rockefeller Center
1230 Avenue of the Americas
New York, NY 10020

FIRESIDE and colophon are registered trademarks of Simon & Schuster Inc.

Designed by Jessica Shatan

Manufactured in the United States of America

1   3   5   7   9   10   8   6   4   2

Library-of Congress Cataloging-in-Publication Data
Carter, Judy.
The homo handbook : getting in touch with your inner homo / Judy Carter.
p.   cm.
Includes bibliographical references and indexes.
1. Coming out (Sexual orientation)—United States.   2. Gays—United States.—Conduct of life.   3. Gays—United
States—Family relationships.   I. Title.
HQ75.16.U6C37   1996
646.7'008'664—dc20   96-20557   CIP

ISBN 0-684-81358-0

Acknowledgments

I'm not a therapist, psychologist, or talk show hostess, and although I know something about coming out from going through the process myself, most of the information in this book comes from the input of over a thousand gay people— some of whom I didn't even sleep with. I would like to thank all who took the time to be interviewed, filled out questionnaires, shared their stories in person and in cyberspace, and mailed me articles—and the cute FedEx girl who delivered them.

Thanks to all the comics, gay and straight, whose jokes appear on these pages, especially Cindy Drummond, Michael Rasky, Michelle Kort, Rob Lotterstein, Joanne Parrent, Barry Steiger, Michael Soares, and Paul Wilson for pizza nights, and to Kathi O'Donohue, who in spite of having nervous breakdowns knows how to get things done.

Much thanks to Ann Glover, Andrea Natalie, and Donelan for their great cartoons and illustrations.

Much gratitude to Kathy Cronin for her wit and wisdom, and to Jed Mattes and his assistant Fred Morris for taking care of the business stuff.

Special thanks and love to stand-up comic Vickie Shaw, whose coming-out courage and humor was a constant reminder of why I am writing this book, and much gratitude to Harriet Katz, cellist of the Ladies Choice String Quartet and writer support extraordinaire. Much appreciation to Chuck Adams for his support and thoughtful editing.

And my heartfelt appreciation to my aunt Edith, who loves me no matter what the others in the synagogue say.

Contents

I prefer to use the word *homo*, *queer*, or *gay* rather than *homosexual*. *Homosexual* is a technical word and sounds more like a science project than a human being.

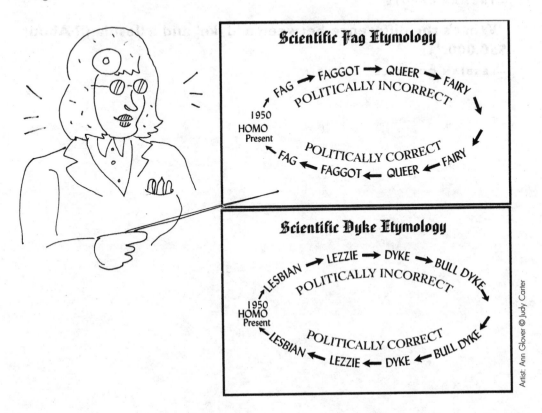

Scientific Fag Etymology

1950 HOMO Present

FAG → FAGGOT → QUEER → FAIRY
POLITICALLY INCORRECT

POLITICALLY CORRECT
FAG ← FAGGOT ← QUEER ← FAIRY

Scientific Dyke Etymology

1950 HOMO Present

LESBIAN → LEZZIE → DYKE → BULL DYKE
POLITICALLY INCORRECT

POLITICALLY CORRECT
LESBIAN ← LEZZIE ← DYKE ← BULL DYKE

Artist: Ann Glover © Judy Carter

And besides, isn't the word HO-MO-SEX-UAL such a *big* word for something most of us do so *little* of the time?

I also choose sometimes to use the word *gay* to include both genders, rather than repeating the phrase *gay and lesbian*. True, there are times when we seem to be worlds apart, but a rigid adherence to *gay and lesbian* seems to divide us into separate camps at a time when we require unity.

Although some of you might perceive *homo* and *queer* as politically incorrect, they work for me precisely because of that connotation. Since they are words that have been used in a derogatory way on every school ground in America—as in, "Don't touch me, you big homo," and "Get out of here, you queer"—using the words ourselves disarms them. By embracing these words, we have gone full circle, transforming what was painful and incorrect into something not only correct but tender—"How's my darling little queer today?"

It's empowering to look into a mirror and say those naughty words. So, this book is for you, you fag, dyke, Mary, butch, fairy, queen, flamer, carpet muncher, fluff diver, queer, you.

"We all know a fag is a homosexual gentleman who has just left the room."
—TRUMAN CAPOTE

"What's the difference between a 'dyke' and a 'lesbian'? About $50,000."
—LESBIAN COMIC LEA DELARIA

Introduction

WHO IS THIS BOOK FOR?

- You, the one reading this book in a gay bookstore, wearing that big hat and phony mustache. It's for you.
- You, in total denial, who bought this book for the recipes. There aren't any.
- You, who bought this book "for a friend," only you don't have any gay friends.
- You, who were given this book by a friend. And you thought you were fooling everyone.
- You, who have very secret fantasies but would never act on them—but have already turned to the chapter on how to get laid.
- You, who married the bride but wanted to honeymoon with the best man.
- You, who were the bride, only to be closer to the groom's mother.
- You, with a gay lifestyle on Saturday night and a straight corporate lifestyle come Monday morning.
- You, who change pronouns when talking to straight people about your lover: "I'm involved with 'them.'"
- You, who have a gay lover but still let your parents fix you up with "that nice blonde."
- You, who go to gay bars but would never go to a gay pride march.
- You, who are out everywhere but can't get laid.

This book is for everyone who's ever spent more time in the closet than it takes to grab a coat, from the flamer to the married woman with three kids who fantasizes about doing other things with her ladies' church group than baking cookies. This book is for you no matter where you are in your journey to be who you are. For the person who has never even thought about coming out, to those who have just begun, this book will give you hope and guidance. To the person who is already out, this book will give you skills to accept yourself fully, sway Rush Limbaugh fans, and zing retorts to stupid hetero remarks. This is your complete *Homo Handbook* on how to be the best homo you can be.

I WAS A HETERO FAILURE

....

My process of becoming a major homo has been long and slow. I didn't come out to myself until I was twenty-eight—I was bogged down with fear, denial, and a bad wardrobe. Before then I was a hetero, only I wasn't very good at it. I tried to be like other girls, I really did. But drag queens walked better in heels than I did. I suffered through aching arches and the deadness of forcing myself to have sex with the wrong gender.

It amazes me how they say that we homos just haven't slept with the right guy/gal. It's ridiculous to think that sleeping with the opposite sex is going to change us. I have slept with men and I know that the opposite usually happens—after sleeping with me, they turn gay.

Truly, for years I slept with a lot of men, trying to find love but always feeling very uncomfortable. Finally I hit hetero bottom. I felt suicidal. At the time I thought *I* was a failure as a woman. I didn't know I was simply a failure at trying to be something I wasn't—straight.

Although sleeping with men always felt wrong, it just didn't occur to me that I was a lesbian. The only visible lesbians were the butch ones, and besides, I didn't bowl. Growing up, I would think, "What is my future mate doing right now?" I never really imagined that "he" was putting on makeup and a bra. I didn't know that I was a normal gay teenager. Of course, it's not like there were a lot of clues. It's not as simple as, When all of us little girls played doctor with one another, I wanted to be the gynecologist. It wasn't that simple.

I equated being gay with going crazy. I was brought up in a "nice Jewish family," programmed to get married and have children. I thought if I ever made love to a woman, I would have to be committed, for it would mean I had gone mad. It is only in looking back that I understand that, sometimes, letting go of who you think you are

Early Signs of Lesbianism

can feel like madness. Sometimes it is necessary to let go of who you're supposed to be in order to find who you really are.

I know it sounds stupid, but it was while watching lesbian singer Holly Near that I consciously realized that I wanted to sleep with a woman—well, actually, I wanted to sleep with Holly Near. She was singing songs about being a lesbian so openly that it made me want to be one—that night, with her. Of course, Holly had other plans that night, none of which included even meeting me. That was the beginning of a conscious change in me, although after my Holly Near wake-up call it took me an entire year to break my lesbian virginity. Hey, I was on the road doing stand-up at Theodore Roosevelt National Park in North Dakota. Let's face it, there weren't many lesbians at the Rough Rider Inn. When I finally did make love with a woman, I still didn't call myself a lesbian. I called myself bisexual or adventurous, or more likely tried to avoid the issue of calling myself anything. The coming-out process is slow.

Five years after that Holly Near concert, I realized that this lesbian thing wasn't a phase, and I outed myself to my mother and my friends. But not at work. Onstage in my stand-up act I still joked about my "boyfriend," until I found lying to be unbearable. My first public coming out was onstage at a concert in Ohio. I was thirty-nine. It had taken me eleven years to have the courage just to publicly admit who I was. At the end the audience jumped to their feet and applauded me. I broke down and cried. My friends held me, assuring me that it was a wonderful show, not understanding why I was so upset. I was crying because after years and years of keeping my sexuality secret, when I let it out, people didn't hate me—they loved me. I was crying for all those senseless years of protecting myself from letting others see the real me. In coming out, I discovered love. In coming out . . . I got dates.

Since then I have come out wherever I work, whether it is a gay-friendly audience in Provincetown or a homophobic "Yahoo, cowboy!" audience deep in the bowels of Texas. My goal is not to let others define who I am. Sometimes I'm accepted, and sometimes I'm greeted with an icy silence or even booed. But even on the difficult nights I know there is always at least one person in the audience who is positively affected by my coming out—and that keeps me going.

As a totally out stand-up comic, I get letters from many people suffering from their secret, "shameful" desires. Being gay in a straight world, most of us grow up wearing a mask—looking outside ourselves to figure out what we are supposed to look like.

I've written this book to give those of you who aren't yet out the courage to go out without any mask on—everywhere. And for those of you major homos who are out everywhere, I've written this book because we all can stand a good laugh and a dose of affirmation. Perhaps if I had picked up this book or one like it, it could have helped me. I wouldn't have wasted the best years of my thighs with the wrong sex. *Coming out*—a gentle process of loving who we are, no matter what the outside world thinks about it.

Who is this book for? This book is for me. Writing this book has been my next step in my process of coming out. In the past year, to every person who has remarked, "This book you're writing, what's it about?" I've had to out myself.

Coming out hasn't been easy for me. Even I, Miss Big Shot Coming-Out Activist, panicked about going so public. In the course of writing this book I was at a ski bar surrounded by beer-drinking college guys. They asked me what I did. I told them I was a writer.

"Oh, what are you writing?"

And I panicked. "A book."

"What's it about?"

Oh, my God, here it goes. If I don't come out, then it means that I'm hiding. So I told them. "It's about coming out," I said and then resisted the desire to add, "Coming out—as a professional skier."

All things considered, I decided it might be inappropriate to write a coming-out book under the pseudonym "J," and so once again I came out. In the course of writing this book I've outed myself to everyone you can imagine: Jehovah's Witnesses, flight attendants, my gardener, neighbors, producers, agents, and my

Orthodox Jewish eighty-two-year-old aunt Edith, who replied, "I love you no matter what you are. But if you're coming out—take a sweater."

Being a major homo is a never-ending challenge. Your coming out can affect the world. When we all come out, they won't be able to tell those lies about us. When we are all out, we won't be those "evil sinners," but we will be Doug, that nice fellow who runs the corner store; Susan, who is my loving friend; Lori, who works next to me; Sam, who is the neighborhood army recruiter; Garry, my neighbor who watches my place when I'm out of town; and Bertha, who delivers my UPS packages.

IMAGINE . . .

- Imagine that you have pictures of you and your lover on your desk at work and nobody cares.

- Imagine that you have become just another ordinary gay person.

- Imagine that you walk down a street hand in hand and no one stares.

- Imagine that you dance with your lover at your office party.

- Imagine that the radical right has to find another group to hate because no one wants to give them money anymore for hating gays.

- Imagine that you are covered by your lover's insurance policy because every state recognizes gay marriages.

- Imagine that there is no longer a need for separate gay churches because religious people realize that loving feels better than hating.

- Imagine that the words *wife* and *husband* are replaced with *life partner.*

- Imagine that a *Wheel of Fortune* contestant introduces her or his life partner to the TV audience.

- Imagine that adoption services don't hesitate to have gay parents adopt.

- Imagine that Hallmark has "To My Mothers on Mother's Day" cards.

Imagine your life. Imagine you have no secrets. Imagine you have no fear. This can be your life. This can be your world.

Step 1: Buy This Book

You've bought a book that has the word *homo* on the cover. Congratulations. In buying this book, you may have accomplished your first step in coming out, or assisted a friend or loved one in acknowledging and accepting themselves. Whether you're a confirmed homo, or "Some of your best friends are gay," or the first person you came out to was the cashier, I want to acknowledge your courage. It doesn't matter whether you felt the need to make up a fictitious research project as your excuse for buying this book or whether you're very advanced and have already scored the cashier's phone number. All that matters is that you are reading a book that will supply you with the tools to make coming out easier and, hopefully, will give you some good yucks along the way.

You might ask yourself: "Of all the things I could be in my life, why would I want to be a major homo?" Well there are advantages.

- **You never have to worry again about who knows you're gay, because everyone does.**
- **You get to go on daytime talk shows.**
- **The only secret you have is how much you weigh.**
- **Straight people will invite you to come liven up their parties.**
- **It's fun having your own float in the gay pride parade.**
- **Other gay people will feel safe to hit on you.**
- **You can run for public office, because you probably are the only candidate not hiding anything.**

- **You don't have to spend all that mental energy figuring out safe pronouns when coworkers ask you about your weekend.**

- **Your boss can't fire you after you come out without being slapped with a sexual-orientation suit.**

- **All that energy it takes to hide can be spent creating a better world.**

Coming out is fun. Straight people don't know what they are missing. Coming out is also challenging, and no one should come out until they are ready. This book is designed to be your support system throughout the tough times. Don't come out without it.

"Pronouns make it hard to keep our sexual orientation a secret when our coworkers ask us about our weekend. 'I had a great weekend with . . . THEM.' Great! Now they don't think you're queer—just a big *slut!*"
—JUDY CARTER

HOW IT WORKS

....

The basic idea of this book is simple: keeping sexual orientation a secret and being so serious about it is harmful to our mental, emotional, and spiritual health. So each chapter in this book contains jokes and a coming-out step. The steps will start small and gradually get more involved. Don't expect to cover all the territory in one day. This isn't Evelyn Wood's speed coming-out course. Coming out is a gradual process of self-discovery, of making small advances a few at a time. You don't have to come out to your mom today, your dad tomor-

row, your boss on Thursday, and *Oprah* on Friday. Coming out is not a race; it's a process. It's not about being the most fabulously out homo, it's about treating yourself with respect.

Coming out wouldn't even be necessary if society didn't automatically assume everyone is straight. The journey of embracing ourselves is a long and difficult one because of all the people along the way who keep telling us who we're supposed to be—and of course we're all supposed to be straight. Parents, teachers, bosses, friends— they all want us to be like them: straight. Sometimes the message is overt and damaging. Sometimes it's subtle . . . and damaging. Tune in to your surroundings and you'll

Stop telling people to "go straight"!

see how all-encompassing this message to conform is, even in subliminal form . . .

"Okay, turn left at the light and then go *straight.*" Drive *straight,* act *straight,* go *straight* to jail and don't collect $200, damn *straight, straighten* up, and the ever popular *Straits* of Gibraltar. Maybe by the time you've finished this book, the next time someone gives you directions to "go straight" you'll look at that fork in the road differently and choose the direction that takes you where you need to go.

WHAT DO YOU NEED TO COME OUT?

Coming-out equipment:

- **Your very own copy of this book, because you're going to be writing in it.**
- **A notebook that will serve as your coming-out journal.**
- **A coming-out buddy. It's very helpful to go through this book step-by-step with another person. Organizing a small group that meets once a week is a great idea too.**
- **Coming-out wardrobe. Get ready, because after coming out you might not want to shop at Wal-Mart.**

> **CAUTION: IF YOU ARE HOLDING THIS BOOK AND CONSIDER YOURSELF STRAIGHT, READ THIS IMMEDIATELY.**

Excuse #1: "I'm not gay. I was just drunk."

It's amazing to me how many people are gay only when they're drunk. Or maybe that means that people are straight only when they're sober. Before we come out we are full of excuses. *I* just thought I wasn't good at finding the

Some people seem to be gay only when they're drunk.

right man. It was a big surprise to find that the right man was . . . a woman. Well, the same surprise could be in store for you. The good news is that you aren't a hetero failure: you could have the makings of a major successful homo!

Whether you view yourself as gay or bisexual or as a "totally straight person," there is some reason why this book is in your hands. It could be the law of synchronicity: we attract to us what we need. Have you been attracting gay people into your life, even if you're "straight"? Is it a coincidence? Is it a coincidence that you are holding a book about this topic at this point in your life? Is it a coincidence that you go to gay bars "for the music"? Good morning!

So, you, holding this book in your hands . . . take the Homo Test in Step 2. The results might surprise you.

Excuse #2: "I'm too old to change."

As if there is a right age to come out! Age is a very popular excuse for not doing anything. "I'm too old to learn to ski." "I'm too old to change my career." "I'm too old to be gay."

In America it seems as if we are supposed to have our lives completely in order by our first high school reunion, and then coast the rest of the way. And yet there are the stories of my friends: Ruth Cummings, who entered medical school at thirty-eight; Beatrice Cole, who took up painting at sixty-seven and became successful at it; Martin Crisp, who at seventy-two started accessorizing.

WHEN ARE PEOPLE OLD? WILL I WAKE UP ONE DAY AND WANT TO WEAR A COAT?

Artist: Ann Glover © Judy Carter

Whether you figured out you were gay at five or not until you were in the retirement home, the truth is that there is no "right" age for being who you are. I met Mary Newman, a grandmother, at a women's conference. At the conference she became attracted to another woman. So, at sixty-four, to her family's shock, she moved out of her husband's house and in with her female lover.

Thinking that you are too old to follow your desires is a *limiting belief*. A limiting belief is often formed in childhood and isn't necessarily based on reality. It is true only because you believe it to be true. "I'm too old, too fat, too busy to come out." In Step 2 you will be asked to examine how your limiting beliefs are keeping you from being happy. The truth of the matter is that change is scary, no matter what age you are, so perhaps the real truth might be that you are not too old to come out, just too scared. Admitting that you are frightened is the first step out of denial. Now comes a choice. Are you going to let fear continue to dictate your life, or are you going to start taking action?

Excuse #3: "It's just a temporary thing. I don't want to call myself gay because I might change my mind."

If you've been in a hetero phase for thirty-four years, how about trying a homo phase for the next thirty-four? Or maybe just one year? How about for today? Seriously, just because you've thought of yourself as straight for a long time doesn't mean that it's too late to change. After all, we all know that it's not how *long* it is that counts, but what you *do* with it. The truth is that the past is gone and you have just today. You might change your mind tomorrow. So what? It does happen. I have a girlfriend who defined herself as a lesbian and was in a lesbian relationship for twelve years. Then she fell in love with Howard. You just never know.

You might be bi, you might be straight, or you might be a major homo. It doesn't matter. The only thing that matters is that you feel free enough to pursue who you are today without the constraints of worrying about tomorrow.

Excuse #4: "If my parents found out, it would kill them."

Although it sounds absurd, it's amazing how many of us feel as if sexual orientation kills. "I can't tell my dad, it will give him a heart attack." Or maybe the real reason is, "I can't come out to my parents; I'll get written out of the will."

Coming out to your parents is hard—especially if they rejected you when you colored your hair fuchsia in eighth grade. If they had trouble with that—after all, it did wash out—how are they going to accept this? Well, they may not. They might reject you. If so, have heart—in Step 7 you will realize that that is not your problem; it's theirs. But if you don't come out, you'll never know. If you don't come out, you're robbing your parents of the opportunity to ever really know you. You're robbing them of an opportunity to love unconditionally.

Coming out to parents is scary. That's why there are those of us who are out at work, out with our friends, out even with strangers—out to everyone except our families. We can be in total queer drag on Halloween yet bring a straight date to our parents' house on Thanksgiving. Then there are those of us whose parents know but never talk about it. The whole family plays the game of "Don't ask, don't tell." So every holiday they invite you and your "special friend" to sleep in the guest room, the one with the bunk beds.

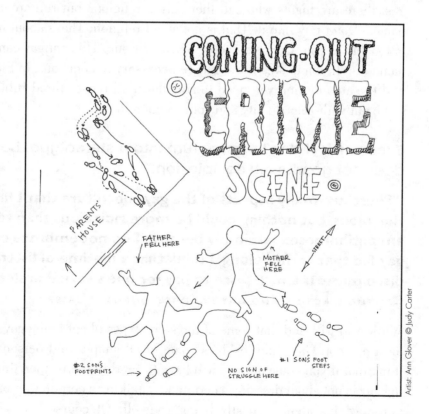

Because it's such a big step, I don't suggest coming out to your parents until you are fairly sure you are ready. In Step 2 you'll learn to feel comfortable with yourself before outing yourself to your parents. Then in Step 7 you'll learn various strategies about coming out to your parents and preparing them for their coming-out process as parents of gay children.

Excuse #5: "It's a mortal sin. The pope says no homos."

Yes, there are bigots who call themselves religious but run around calling us names. Don't buy into it. That is not about religion. That's about hate. Your relationship to your God is a deeply personal issue. This antigay campaign in the name of religion makes it even more necessary to come out. In Step 9 you will find the ammunition you need to zing down all those stupid Bible quotes and come out with your dignity and your religion intact.

Excuse #6: "I don't want to turn into a stereotype. Lavender does not go with my complexion."

"There are many aspects of the gay subculture that I find ridiculous, but nothing could be more ridiculous than to say that I am antihomosexual simply because I do not embrace every twitty gay fad that comes along. I think that a lifetime of listening to disco music is a high price to pay for one's sexual preference."
—AUTHOR, ACTOR, AND GAY ACTIVIST QUENTIN CRISP

While you will find that some of the stereotypes about being gay are accurate, most are not. Gays and lesbians come in all shapes and personalities. If you think that if you come out you will have to act differently, then think again. Being gay is not about dressing a certain way, talking a certain way, or acting a certain way. It's about honestly being yourself. Of course, *yourself* might just surprise you. You just may find yourself acting more authentically as you discard your phony, hetero persona. Just relax and excuse yourself while you slip into something a little more gay.

"I can't help looking gay. I put on a dress and people say, 'Who's the dyke in the dress?'"
—COMIC KAREN RIPLEY

Excuse #7: "My life works just fine without telling people everything."

I say if something works, then don't change it. But is there a possibility that your life doesn't really work as well as you would like, or that it could work even better if you weren't carrying secrets and leading a double life? Lying has an effect on you.

"But I'm not really lying. I just don't like to discuss my personal life."

A lie has to do with conveying a false image or impression. Because heteros assume you are one of them unless you tell them you're not, you are lying. By your omission, you are really saying that there is something wrong with your life, and people will pick up on it. They won't know what it is, but there will be something about you that pushes people away. Even if there is only one person whom you are frightened to be yourself in front of, you are living in some degree of self-hate, and that's bound to affect your success and happiness.

Excuse #8: "I can't come out at work. I'll be fired."

Many people think coming out at work would be trading your pink triangle for a pink slip. Yet there are a lot of people who are out at work and are totally accepted. Step 8 will prepare you for coming out to your boss, and if you don't have a job yet, it will give you tips on finding a job where you don't have to hide your sexual orientation.

Excuse #9: "I can't be gay, because I want to have a family."

Gay people can have families. You don't need to marry a breeder to do this. There are surrogates, sperm banks, and adoption. If there is a will there is a way—and if you have ova, you can find a donor—and a turkey baster.

WHAT? EVERYTHING'S FROZEN? DON'T YOU HAVE ANYTHING FRESH?

SPERM BANK

Artist: Ann Glover © Judy Carter

Judy's grandma goes to a sperm bank.

In Step 7 you will see that two men or two women can have children and live just like *The Dick Van Dyke Show,* or maybe *The Dick Dyke Dyke Show.*

Excuse #10: "I worry about gay bashing. I worry about losing my kids."

Gay bashing does happen. In some states, gay people do lose their kids. These are real concerns. In Step 2 you will learn that there are realistic fears and fantasized fears, and you will learn the difference. That's why this book can help you learn to come out without jeopardizing your health or well-being. And in Step 10 you'll be encouraged to become a gay activist and change the laws!

Excuse #11: "If I come out, my straight friends will reject me."

Hey, miss, you live in a one-bedroom apartment with your gym teacher. Like, they don't know. Wake up and smell the coffee!

It's a gift to be gay. What, such a gift I want to return? Most people live their lives without any self-examination. Being gay, we are

9:00 THE DYKES OF HAZZARD
9:30 DESIRING WOMEN
10:00 MARRIED,... WITH POODLES
10:30 LEAVE IT TO BEAVER

FAMILY NIGHT ON GAY T.V.

Artist: Ann Glover © Judy Carter

forced to look at ourselves, and through that self-examination—although it's painful—we can open channels to a higher consciousness of living.

"I don't know if one ever fully gets used to or accepts their sexuality. Hets smugly think they do, but only because they haven't ever thought to question it—but for queers, there always is a time where one deals with what they are."

—WRITER BRAD SHAPCOTT

"I've decided! . . . I'm Gay . . . I'm happy about it . . . and you'll all just have to deal with it!"

Hey, if your friends reject you because you are honest with them, then they might be *toxic friends,* and in Step 6 you'll learn how to dump them.

Excuse #12: "There is no need for me to come out. I'm already out everywhere."

Some of you might think that you have already come out. I beg to differ. It's not something that you do once and it's over. Coming out is a never-ending process of fully accepting who you are and coming out of hiding. Coming out is having the willingness to be who you are no matter the consequences.

There you are on a plane, reading *Rubyfruit Jungle.* The man sitting next to you as you cross the international date line is reading Rush Limbaugh's new book. He asks what your book is about. You're tired; you don't want to deal with it. You say: "Oh, it's all about gardening."

Coming out is a never-ending process for all of us. There will always be another opportunity for us to take a risk and take a stand for who we truly are.

So even you, the gay activist, read on. It might surprise you to find that you still have some forgotten items hiding in your closet.

Excuse #13: "I want bridal presents."

Me too. So when you want to settle down, have a commitment ceremony and get those gifts. And hey, if you get tired of buying gifts for hetero showers, next time when you go to a shower, don't give a gift—buy one for yourself. Homos deserve Cuisinarts too!

"What's a bridal shower if you're gay? It's the parade of gifts that you'll never get 'cause *you're* a homosexual! 'Come in and take a look at the blender, toaster, silverware *you'll* have to buy yourself!!!' I hate that. I don't bring a gift anymore, I *take* one. I have six Cuisinarts. I don't give a shit . . . they *owe* us."
—LESBIAN COMIC SUZANNE WESTENHOFFER

CARTER'S COMING-OUT STRATEGY

In coming out to a world that is frequently hostile, we can often feel powerless. With all those stupid antigay propositions, it sometimes feels as if "they" are making war on us. As in any war, each side strategizes its moves. A side that simply reacts is the side that loses. A solution is for us to create our own coming-out strategy, our coming-out plan, in which there are no losers.

Carter's Coming-Out Strategy teaches you to create a support system for yourself before coming out to others. Just as you wouldn't jump out of a plane without a parachute, you don't need to come out and put yourself in financial or emotional jeopardy. You'll come out one step at a time, and with each step there will be a strategy to minimize the potential risk.

First, come out to yourself and feel comfortable *before* you come out to friends. Next, come out to friends who provide an emotional support system *before* you come out to your parents. And then come out to a good lawyer *before* you come out to the U.S. Army. There will always be fear, but you will find, if you follow this book, that fear can turn into excitement as you discover the freedom of being who you are.

Steps

This book is divided into ten steps. Each step has one major coming-out objective. The order in which I present these steps is not necessarily the right order for *your* coming-out process. It's merely my idealized version and should be individualized. You need to proceed in a way that feels right for you. But since I'm the author, I get to lay it out the way I think it should be done. As many of my lovers would be quick to tell you, I'm not always right, but I've always got a plan. In actuality, these steps overlap and can be done in any order. Some people come out to one parent but not to the other until years later. Some people are

totally out at work (because they work for the gay and lesbian center) and closeted with their family. Some people have many lovers way before considering
themselves gay, while others totally identify themselves as gay but their only
sexual experience was locking eyes with their gym teacher.

Read each step even if you think, "Been there, done that." It might surprise
you that there is still more to do.

Tests

Throughout this book there will be pop quizzes. Don't worry, you don't have to
study for them any more than you ladies would study for a Pap smear. Some of
the tests are serious, and most are fun. They are a way for you to have a direct
experience with this book. I suggest writing directly into the book . . . in pen. I
know all of you anal retentives are sweating now: "But what if I make a mistake?"

There is no way to make mistakes. Commit to your coming-out process and
have fun messing up this book. Your friends can get their own copy. Codependent no more!

Journal Workshops

During each step you will be asked to make journal entries. Keep a separate
notebook for this; it will be used along with this book. Be spontaneous. Write as
quickly as possible and don't take time to edit yourself. Let your thoughts and
feelings flow, and know that there is no such thing as a wrong feeling or thought.
We frequently tend to overanalyze ourselves and end up filtering out what's
really going on. Unless you're Heidi Fleiss or former senator Bob Packwood,
chances are your journal is not going to get published or reviewed. Journal writing is simply a technique for you to get in touch with your feelings.

If you find yourself blocked, keep writing anyway, and eventually something
true will emerge and get you past the blockage. It's a shame how many people
stop writing *before* getting to the stuff worth writing about.

Stretches

At the end of each chapter, you will be asked to do a Stretch. In exercise,
stretching is a powerful tool to give you flexibility. As in physical stretching,
where it feels that if you reach any further you will break, so it is with coming-
out Stretches. You might feel the fear of falling apart, of going beyond what
you've known to be safe, but with every Stretch you'll find new strength. With
stretching, if you hold at the place where it's really painful, you eventually ease

up and can stretch a little further. Just as you might not be able to touch your toes right now, by Step 9 you might be amazed at the comfort you feel touching Republicans.

Some Stretches will be easy and some will make you ache. To the person who is just coming out of denial, a Stretch is buying this book, while to a major homo, out in the world, a stretch might be coming out while appearing on *Jeopardy*.

Do you remember the first time you rode on a bike without training wheels? There was no half-assed way to do it. Maybe someone held the bike as you got on, but there had to be that moment when that other person let go and you took the risk of falling. All risks are essentially about falling: falling out of a job, out of a relationship, out of safety.

Stretches are about trust. The person you need to trust 100 percent is yourself—your instincts, your strengths, your ability to survive negativity. You must trust the strength that lies underneath all your hesitations about coming out.

When the fear comes up during these Stretches you will need to call forth this trust. Who was it that got you to ride the bike? Was it your father, or maybe your mother, whom you trusted? Your whole body told you that you might fall, but you trusted someone enough to take the risk. As adults, we have to rely on ourselves. Some people give a name to that kind of faith—they call it God. That word is going to be mentioned in this book, and it's a difficult word for many of us because that name has been used so often to condemn us. So to take some of the awkwardness away, for now, I'm going to refer to God as Big Bertha.

Right now my heart is beating and I don't have to think, "Go, heart, beat." It is out of my control, and I trust that whatever is making my heart beat is taking care of me when no one else seems to. In coming out, you will need to depend on that force, whether you call it God, or a Higher Power, or just plain old Big Bertha.

JOURNAL WORKSHOP—How Comfortable Are You?

Answer the following questions, and remember to write as quickly as possible. This is not an intellectual exercise. This is not a test. Be spontaneous. (This is very important.) Do not censure your thoughts. Write without taking your hand from the page.

1. How did you *feel* when you bought this book?

2. Did you hide it from other customers?

3. If you felt uncomfortable, what did you think others were thinking?

4. What are your excuses for not coming out?

5. What are your biggest fears of what will happen if you do?

6. How do you feel about calling yourself gay, lesbian, or just plain homo?

7. At this point, whom are you willing to come out to?

8. Whom won't you tell?

STRETCH: Going Public

1. **Take this book and read it in a public place with the cover showing (for example, a library, a park, a bus stop). Write down in your coming-out journal how it made you feel.**

2. **Go through one day and count how many times you lie about your sexuality. This includes how many times you omit telling the whole truth. Write in your coming-out journal what the lies were and how they affected you.**

3. **Give this book as a gift to someone you suspect of being in the closet. Then go buy another one. (I have no personal gain from this. Right!)**

Step 2: Come Out to Yourself

"To love oneself is the beginning of a lifelong romance."

—OSCAR WILDE

The first person who needs to acknowledge and accept you is—you. So, are you gay? Let's find out. Take the Homo Test.

THE HOMO TEST

Men

❏ Do you want to sleep with other men? (If you've checked this one, go directly to Step 3. You're a fag.)

❏ Can you name all the actors who played Tarzan?

❏ Do you use the word *fabulous* more than five times a day?

❏ Do you encourage your girlfriend to let her mustache grow in?

❏ Do you scour the TV listings looking for old Tab Hunter flicks?

❏ Was changing clothes in junior high P.E. more fun than the actual sport?

❏ Is trying to fit "Yo, dude!" into your vocabulary like trying to master a foreign tongue?

❏ While growing up did you play with Barbies?

❏ While growing up did you want to be Barbie?

❏ And did you want to marry Ken?

❏ Do you know all the songs from more than five Broadway musicals?

❏ Do you consider Mary Kay a career choice?

❏ Super Bowl? What's that?

Women

❑ Do you work for Federal Express? (If you've checked this one, go right to Step 3. You're a dyke.)

❑ Have you seen every Jodie Foster film?

❑ Do you have a first edition copy of *The Well of Loneliness* by Radclyffe Hall?

❑ Does flannel make you excited?

❑ Do you find yourself at golf tournaments but don't play golf?

❑ Do you have a large quantity of sensible shoes?

❑ Did you have a crush on your gym teacher?

❑ Are you a gym teacher?

❑ Are you currently living in a one-bedroom apartment with your gym teacher?

❑ Do you bowl?

❑ Can't talk, the Super Bowl is on.

"You know you're gay when you find yourself friends with Elizabeth Taylor and Madonna."
—GAY COMIC BOB SMITH

Okay, I'm having fun with stereotypes, but the truth is, if you took this test you probably are gay. And if you took the test in pen . . . big news flash . . . you're definitely queer!

"Oh no, I'm not a homo," you say?

Just the fact that you are reading this means that *gay* is an issue for you. Even if you have never acted on any gay fantasies, have hetero fantasies, or are bisexual, as far as this book is concerned, you qualify as a homo. If there weren't homophobia, we wouldn't be having such problems with these labels. We wouldn't think twice about being a big queer, but because of homophobia all sexuality is reduced to one word. And according to a survey of ten top homophobes, that one and only word is STRAIGHT.

Isn't it homophobia that tells us that there is only one right way to make love, and that everything else is wrong? Well, put that out of your mind for a while, and for the next several pages don't listen to it. Ideally, your sexuality should be like your eye color—no big thing. But that's not the way it is. In fact, being what most people refer to as

"If you guys don't mind, I think I'll stay just plain gay."

gay might be bigger than you think. One's sexuality is too big to put into one small word. We have narrow terms to work with—*gay, lesbian, bisexual*—but as you read this book you will see that there are so many types of gays, or as my grandmother calls us (use your best Yiddish accent here), "*ch*omosextionals." (Clear your throat on the *CH*.) There are bisexuals, bull dykes, lipstick lesbians, butch fags, butches, femmes, femmy butches, butchy fems, pillow princesses, tops, bottoms, celibate gays, and priests.

Putting all gay people into one category is like putting all straight people into one category. It doesn't really work, does it? There is not one kind of gay. Just as each snowflake is different, so is every queen.

I wonder, if there were no homophobia, how many people who call themselves straight would identify as gay. If there weren't homophobia, how many bisexuals would identify as gay?

CARTER'S STATUTE OF LIMITATIONS ON BEING BISEXUAL

••

This is arbitrary and certainly politically incorrect, but I'm going to set a statute of limitations on being bisexual. Of course, there really are some of us out there who really do enjoy sex with either gender. But a great many of us call ourselves bisexual when in fact, while we may be able to perform with either sex, we have a definite preference for one or the other. It's those guys and gals I'm writing my rule for. You can call yourself bisexual until you make up your mind. But if you've been dating your own gender for three years . . . face it, you're gay! I'm not saying that you can't change your mind and be straight again, but for now . . . you're gay. Deal with it!

"My bisexual dilemma was that my gay friends thought I'm a lesbian in denial and my straight friends thought . . . I'm a lesbian in denial."
—LESBIAN COMIC LACIE HARMON

Artist: Ann Glover; Writer: Brent Capps

Stop being afraid! Stop being ashamed! It's not about sex. It's about who you feel free to love and be loved by. Reducing us to a sexual issue creates shame and sends us into denial. How can we have pride when we feel everyone looks at us solely as sexual?

How can we ask others to accept and love us when we hate ourselves? How can we educate others when we have contempt for who we are?

"So many women can't say the word *lesbian* even when their mouth is full of one."
—LESBIAN COMIC KATE CLINTON

The goal of Step 2 is to get us to come out of denial, come out of shame, and come into pride. It's time to stop letting others define us. It's time to do a high colonic and get toxic homophobia out of our own system. In this chapter we are going to hose out the fear, the self-hate, the bullshit. Life is not about sex, hate, fear; it's about love. It's time to start loving ourselves.

"That word *lesbian* sounds like a disease. And straight men know because they're sure that they're the cure."
—LESBIAN COMIC DENISE MCCANLES

COMING-OUT-OF-DENIAL TEST

"I'm not like those people."
Check all that apply to you.

❏ I'm going through a phase.

❏ I'm just experiencing a reaction to a disturbing childhood.

❏ I'm not really gay (but my lover is).

❏ I'm not gay (I'm just in love with one person, who happens to be the same sex).

❏ I don't look gay.

❏ I'm married with children.

❏ (*Men*) I was just horny and there were no women in the park that day.

❏ (*Women*) I slept with that woman because my boyfriend always said it was one of his fantasies (even though we broke up three years ago).

❏ I've had sex with a lot of people of the opposite sex.

❏ I don't want to label myself.

❏ I'm not a lesbian; I'm a feminist.

❏ I'm bisexual.

❏ For Big Bertha's sake, I'm a man of the cloth!

JOURNAL WORKSHOP: "If I'm gay, that means . . ."

Look over what you checked off, and write in your coming-out journal, "If I am gay, that means . . ."

Writing as quickly as possible, put down what it means to you to be gay. Does it mean that you will never have children? That you will lose your friends? That you will have to dress funny? That you will choreograph a major Broadway musical?

HOW DOES HOMOPHOBIA AFFECT YOU?

Homophobia is a hatred of gay people based in fear. It affects all of us living in this society—straight and gay—manifested as a hate that permeates every segment of society. In kindergarten we hear the word *queer*. We see states pass laws against us. We hear people tell us we are going to hell, all in the name of God (I mean Big Bertha).

How can we not be affected by all of this hate? It hurts us on a deeply internal level. Whether we like it or not, the ugliness of homophobia affects our lives and our actions. This hatred is so all-pervasive that it can seep into our own psyches, keeping us in hiding as we let fear control us.

Homophobia teaches others to hate us and teaches us to hate ourselves, to be ashamed of who we are. But before we can escape this shame, we have to admit we feel it.

TEST: ARE YOU HOMOPHOBIC?

The Negative-Stereotype Checklist

Check all that you think apply to gay people. Go through this list as quickly as possible, without pondering your responses. Be quick and honest.

Lesbians

❏ are mostly militant and shout a lot

❏ hate men

❏ have penis envy

❏ like seducing straight, feminine women

❏ have mostly blue-collar jobs

❏ are never ballerinas, supermodels, or movie stars

❏ are mostly lonely women

❏ know how to change a carburetor but not baby diapers

- ❏ are mostly alcoholics and never drink beer out of a glass
- ❏ are mostly butch
- ❏ shop for their wardrobe at Sears
- ❏ get their hair cut by a barber or at Super Cuts
- ❏ don't wear makeup
- ❏ mostly all own motorcycles
- ❏ travel in packs of softball teams
- ❏ are good at sports but especially bowling, softball, volleyball, golf, and basketball

- ❏ are angry
- ❏ live in secrecy
- ❏ don't have families or children
- ❏ are rejected
- ❏ are in need of therapy
- ❏ have been sexually molested
- ❏ have had bad childhoods
- ❏ are hard women

© Donelan

Gay Men

- ❏ don't have long-term relationships
- ❏ are very promiscuous
- ❏ are very lonely
- ❏ are victims of bad childhoods
- ❏ are losers in life
- ❏ live in secrecy
- ❏ care more about getting laid than having a relationship
- ❏ like to dress in women's clothing
- ❏ are mostly nelly sissies who think *fuel injection engine* describes a hot date
- ❏ are never car mechanics, drill sergeants, or macho movie stars
- ❏ don't have families or children
- ❏ are in need of therapy

- ❏ are feminine and not very aggressive
- ❏ all know how to cook
- ❏ are big criers, especially when watching a Judy Garland movie
- ❏ love to trash others in a bitchy way

© Donelan

❏ snap their fingers a lot and say, "You go, girl!"

❏ like helping young schoolboys with their homework

❏ don't excel in sports except certain water sports

❏ lisp and have high, effeminate voices

❏ go through the Indiana Jones ride at Disneyland just for the possibility that they will be whipped

❏ all want to be Barbra Streisand

Add any more negative stereotypes you have of gay people (*Gay people are poor, too sexual,* and so on):

❏ _____   ❏ _____

❏ _____   ❏ _____

❏ _____   ❏ _____

❏ _____   ❏ _____

Stereotypes are stupid and dangerous myths that make others afraid to know us and make us afraid to know ourselves. Sometimes they can be fun, and I'm certainly using them in this book as a source of humor, but in the wrong hands they can be dangerous, especially when they are used to keep us in hiding.

Stereotypes helped to keep me in the closet for a long time. One of the main reasons it was hard for me to accept that I was gay was that I didn't fit the stereotypes; certainly I was not like the dykes I saw on *Oprah.* In the eighties, the only lesbians who were visible were the ones who couldn't hide. There weren't any out femmes, so the lesbians who went on TV were women who looked as if they never had a good hair day in their life. I wasn't one of *them.* Recently, thank Bertha, we've been able to get past the extreme image of lesbians and have made the world realize that we come in all shapes and sizes, all colors and varieties. How wonderful to be out, and how ridiculous most stereotypes are. I can wear dresses *and* Doc Martens.

Look over the stereotypes on the checklist. If you've checked any of them or harbor any other antigay ones yourself, then you might have something to think about.

TEST: ARE YOU "POSITIVELY" GAY?

It seems as if being gay puts us in the situation of having to constantly react to hatred. It takes a toll on one's self-esteem always to be put in a defensive position. We end up shouting our pride rather than quietly acknowledging it. But what if there were no homophobia? How then would you define yourself? How would your life be different? Would you be more open at work, or would you still have feelings of not fitting in? Would you be more affectionate with your lover in public, or are you just not a hand-holding type of person anyway?

In this test I ask you to sit quietly where you won't be disturbed. Maybe even turn the phone off. Take a deep breath, hold it, then let it out on a count of five. Close your eyes, listen, and focus on your breathing. Do this until you feel relaxed. Then open your eyes and go over this list, checking items that apply to you.

I am . . .

❏ loving	❏ enthusiastic	❏ fun
❏ caring	❏ loyal	❏ funny
❏ trustworthy	❏ faithful	❏ talented
❏ feeling	❏ devoted	❏ exciting
❏ passionate	❏ religious	❏ smart
❏ sensuous	❏ spiritual	❏ interesting

I hope that you checked at least one item in the above list. If you didn't, you're going to need to move out of your parents' home, stop reading Sylvia Plath, and realize what a wonderful person you are.

Now, turn to the list of negative gay stereotypes on page 34. Did you check items there?

Looking over these last two lists, ask yourself: Where do you mostly live? The truth is that whether we are gay or straight, we all live in a mixed list. We love ourselves *and* hate our thighs. We are spiritual *and* we watch *Wheel of Fortune.* We are smart *and* we go to bed with idiots. Yet how many of us live our lives fo-

cusing solely on the negatives! I have a critic inside me that constantly informs me I'm fat, mean, and not funny. The way I used to treat my inner child, I could have been arrested for child abuse.

Artist: Ann Glover © Judy Carter

STRETCH: The "Bad" Words Workshop

Look into a mirror and call yourself all the "bad" words you've heard us called. Say them in the way a homophobe might say them to you: "You faggot." "You big dyke."

Try it.

Now turn it all around and say it as if it were the most loving compliment you could ever give yourself: "My sweet little homo." "You beautiful diesel dyke." "You masculine, sexy faggot." "You are so dykey and sexy in those combat boots."

Add any others that you can think of.

JOURNAL WORKSHOP: What Does Homophobia Feel Like?

Now answer these questions:

1. **How does the word *fag* make you feel?**

2. **How does calling yourself a *dyke* make you feel?**

3. **Write in your coming-out journal what this Stretch brought up for you. Write as much as you can and be spontaneous, putting down whatever comes into your head without censoring any of it.**

JOURNAL WORKSHOP: Affirmations

Affirmations are a powerful way to embrace the totality of who we are. They work even if you don't consciously believe them. They resonate on a subconscious level and create success. Or maybe I'm just from California. But try it anyway.

Look over the "positively gay" list on page 37 and pick three items you didn't check or didn't think of. Arrange them into a sentence such as

I am a loving, trusting, powerful man/woman!

Write your affirmation here:

_____

Say your affirmation ten times a day, even if you don't believe it at first. Write it down in a place you will see it each morning. Make this affirmation a contract with yourself. Say it before you go to sleep each night. Write it at least once every day. One day you just might realize you have become that person.

"Growing up, I always thought that I'd marry a rich, athletic man. Now *I'm* making money and jogging. I guess I've become the man I thought I wanted to marry."
—JUDY CARTER

By affirming the positives we are not only changing ourselves but creating a ripple effect that can change the world. And it takes a lot of affirming to transform all the negativity coming at us. Let's look at what happens when we let the negatives rule our lives.

BEING NEGATIVELY GAY

Let's just say that you have a limiting belief that if you come out at work, you'll be fired.

Limiting belief: Coming out at work is bad.

Even though you are totally capable at your job, perhaps even brilliant, a part of you chooses to believe that who you really are is unacceptable, and therefore you keep that a secret.

Look at the ripple effect of this belief. You don't participate when others talk about their relationships. You go to the Christmas party alone. You begin to feel isolated. You begin to dislike others for not being more friendly to you. By keeping your sexuality a secret, on some level you are communicating, "I'm not a worthy human being." Then you don't get a promotion. You don't get invited out.

Who created all of this fear and suspicion? Was it them or was it you? By examining your limiting beliefs, you can actually change your and others' realities—maybe not overnight, but before the government balances the budget.

REALISTIC FEARS VERSUS IMAGINED FEARS

In coming out you will face fear. Some of these fears are realistic and others are imagined. There was a study done on how college students handle fear of failure when taking finals. It found that there were two types of students. There were students who would exaggerate the outcome of fearful situations, and there were students who were more realistic. While one group acknowledged that there was a chance of failure and that there would be certain ramifications from failing, they also acknowledged that there were solutions: they could take the test over; they could repeat the course; they could make changes in their major; and so on. The other group felt that if they failed their final they would die.

How many of us feel that, if we come out to everyone, death awaits us? Us or someone we love. Many of us tend to visualize the wreckage of our future: "If I come out to my boss, he/she will hate me, I'll lose my job, I'll be broke, I'll go homeless, I'll live in the streets, I'll starve to death."

Yes, there are realistic coming-out fears. Your boss *may* fire you. Your parents *may* reject you. But sometimes we are so overwhelmed with fear that we don't ask ourselves important questions:

- **Do I want to work for a boss who is so homophobic?**
- **Would I be happier working in an environment where I could be who I am?**
- **Would telling my parents create an opportunity for them to start changing their limiting beliefs, and bring us closer?**
- **Do I want the fear of what *might* happen rule my life?**

Some of the consequences of coming out might scare you, but some might be only imagined. Holding hands in public with your lover in Tuscaloosa, Alabama, might produce a reaction different than in West Hollywood. But if you're frightened to hold hands in West Hollywood, you might need to examine your fears. In some situations you need to be more realistic and exercise caution . . . and maybe move out of Tuscaloosa.

JOURNAL WORKSHOP: Fear Reality Check

1. **Write down your fears about coming out in your coming-out journal (for example, lose job, lose parents, lose my mind . . .).**

2. **Write out your worst-case scenario.**

3. **Now look over your fears and try to turn them around. Can you put a positive spin on even your most negative scenario?**

4. **Now look over your writings and arrange your fears in order of reality. (Score 10 for the most realistic fears and 1 for the acid-trip ones.)**

STRETCH: Mini-Outing

Name a few people in your life whom you know to be absolutely gay friendly. It could be your gay hairdresser, or your aunt Naomi, who plays center field on her women's softball team. What would be the worst consequence of coming out to them? Is it realistic to be frightened of coming out to them? Can you consider simply talking to them about the subject of sexual orientation? Can you come out to them? The worst thing that could happen is that they might introduce you to someone.

WHY HOMOPHOBIA?

....

Bigots say that gays and lesbians are evil sinners who want to convert children to a life of homosexuality. That's an interesting myth, given that most of us come from straight parents. It's not true; in fact it's laughable. So why does it exist?

"Most of our parents are straight. Heteros who hate us should quit having us."
—LESBIAN COMIC LYNDA MONTGOMERY

Religion, government, and political movements have always used fear to control the masses. In order to build a power base, an enemy needs to be created. Stereotypes are used to stigmatize the enemy. It's no wonder that the antigay movement uses language very similar to that used in Hitler's anti-Jew campaign or McCarthy's anticommunist campaign. Just take a look at all the millions of dollars collected in response to the Christian Coalition's stop-the-gay-agenda campaign.

Because so many of us agree to hide, to be invisible, we have become (as the bigots call us) the perfect "enemy among us."

But on the other hand, studies have shown that once people meet and get to know gay people, their stereotypes and beliefs begin to fade. You might not want to come out in a gay pride march, but you might

Artist: Ann Glover © Judy Carter

be more effective coming out in your personal life to people. In coming out we become real human beings and lose our standing as faceless objects of hate. Hate loses its potency when people have to give us a face, a personality, when we become someone's relative, someone's friend, someone's lover—in short, just another person. People need to know that the only agenda we have is to be treated with respect and dignity.

DON'T ASK, DON'T TELL

Don't ask, don't tell. This is the unwritten rule that has kept us in hiding from our friends, family, coworkers, and even one another. This rule is a message to both gays and straights. The straights are not supposed to ask, and we are not supposed to tell. When I first came out to friends, their response was that they had known for years that I was gay. The problem was that they didn't know how to *ask* me and I didn't know how to *tell* them. Until I did come out, I didn't really realize how distant I was from others, nor did I know the extent of my isolation. I felt left out as I watched everyone else in my family bring their partners to holiday dinners. Playing the senseless game of "Don't ask, don't tell," I lied or evaded personal questions; that created distance between me and my family. What an energy saver it is to be out! Now, when a relative *asks* me whom I'm dating, I simply *tell* them the truth: "I'm dating Kathy, Margot, and an awesome right fielder on my women's softball team named Jane. Yes, Mom, I'm not only playing the field . . . I'm dating it!"

Has every relative and friend embraced me "despite" my being gay? No, but Aunt Sylvia's Passover seders weren't that much fun to begin with. Coming out might be a bit easier if I were dating girls named Pat, Lee, or Bernie.

"Don't ask, don't tell" kills love and keeps us in dysfunction. My family lived by this rule in all arenas. Of course I couldn't tell them I was gay. I couldn't even tell them I had a C in math. I had to keep everything a secret. I smiled through my life, performing the role of who I was supposed to be so my presence wouldn't upset anyone. I was so busy hiding so much of myself to please others that I denied them the challenge and, yes, the beauty of truly knowing me. And I deprived myself too. If you don't let people know you're gay, you're also not letting them know that you are a loving, creative person. Human beings are not so compartmentalized. When we cut out a "small" part of ourselves, we are removing our love for ourselves and for others. You might have brainwashed yourself to think that you are protecting others, but the truth is, you are damaging yourself.

JOURNAL WORKSHOP: Don't Ask, Don't Tell

1. **List below five instances in the past week when someone didn't ask and you didn't tell (for example:** *When a coworker asked about my weekend*).

_____

_____

_____

_____

_____

2. **What did you lose by not telling?**

3. **What positive effects could telling have on your relationships?**

4. **Is there anyone on this list you might consider telling? Today?**

STRETCH: Just How Much Do You Lie?

Go just one day without telling any lies, exaggerations, or half-truths. Just how honest are you when your coworker asks you, *"Who did you go out with last night?"*

Or when your mom asks you, *"Did you like that gift I bought you?"*

Or when your lover asks you, *"I love you. Do you* really *love me?"*

At the end of the day write in your journal how successful or unsuccessful you were at telling the truth. I was surprised just how much I lie—though I admit I cut myself some slack. After all, I'm doing pretty good for someone who's only twenty-eight years old and weighs only 105 pounds. Right! In my dreams!

COMING OUT OF SEXUAL SHAME
....

Another result of homophobia is to become frightened of our very own sexual energy. Sexual energy is with us our whole life. Despite Madison Avenue stereotypes, sexuality doesn't depend on how firm you are, how rich you are, or how big or small certain parts of you are. It doesn't even require another person in bed with you to feel it. It's an energy that we're all born with. It's an energy that inspires us, not only to make love but to write, paint, dance, and create. And to the extent that we allow ourselves to feel it and express it, it's an energy that makes us desired, adored, and HOT!

As children, gay and straight, we all naturally experienced the full pulsation of life until someone told us that we were wrong. "Don't touch that! You're being bad!"

Being gay, however, we got a double dose of negativity. Certain words on the playground seemed reserved just for us: "Hey . . . queer, lezzie, fairy."

We quickly learned that if we were to be loved and approved of, certain natural behavior had to extinguished. So even as children we learned to police our own emotions, sending our playfulness, our impulsiveness, our sexuality into a corner. Growing up we learned to control and even deny our natural desires, rather than give them expression. As a result we have often become adults who are controlling, self-censoring, and ultimately shut down.

I remember at eight years old being labeled too physical and being called a lezzie when playing with my girlfriends. So I learned to control myself and stopped playing that way. What had seemed natural and spontaneous fun to a child was suddenly a bad thing, something to be avoided. When I was a teenager, this repression affected all aspects of my creative expression. No wonder that in high school plays I got the old-woman parts. At sixteen, when I should have been the sexy ingenue, I was playing Golda in *Fiddler*.

Even after I started having women lovers, I was still unaware of just how much I was suffering from sexual suppression. Since I was still somewhat detached emotionally from my sexual energies, I was under the assumption that I needed to *have* sex in order to *feel* sexual. Thinking that my sexual energy existed only when I was in relationship to another person made me into sort of a sexual vampire, sucking off others' sexual energy and moving on when I'd depleted them. And boy, if that isn't attractive. I mean, have you ever overheard someone at a party saying, "Look at the desperate, needy person over there . . . she's so hot!"?

Coming out of shame about my sexuality and reclaiming ownership has been a very challenging, continuous process. How wonderful to know that sexual power is something that's abundant inside of me! Sure, I have my bad days, times when I feel just about as desirable as a cow in heat. But, letting go of the walls I built to protect myself, I'm creating more and more days when I feel alive and passionate. Since coming out and embracing my sexuality, I'm no longer frightened of roller coasters or the thrill of an unexpected hand on my thigh. They are both fun to ride.

JOURNAL WORKSHOP: Exploring Your Sexual Energy

1. **When do you first recall feeling bad or shameful about your sexuality? Write about the event that caused it and how it made you feel.**

2. **Lie down, close your eyes, and imagine your earliest sensation of feeling sexually free, of feeling confident about your body. It could be a time in childhood when you felt strong, confidently naked, beautiful . . . Write a description of how that felt.**

STRETCH: Come Out to Your Body

Breathe. Note that when feeling scared you usually hold your breath on the inhale. You are holding in the feeling. Those moments build up until we have such a large collection of stuffed feelings we could open up a store.

A slow, long breath in and a giant deep exhale release tensions and put you in touch with your body.

Practice today. Make a note to breathe when you sit down at your desk, when speaking to another person. That's why cigarettes are so effective in bar conversations. They give one an excuse to breathe in and out. Sometimes people feel

Store of Stuffed Feelings

stupid just taking in a big inhale, and they exhale while speaking to another person. Try it without a cigarette, though. That way there are fewer negative side effects to breathing. When someone asks you a question, don't answer right away. Breathe in, let it out, and feel the relaxation happen in your body.

My ex-lover smokes, and in the middle of doing chores she would regularly take cigarette breaks, when she would go outside and walk around smoking. I don't smoke, but I wanted to take a break from my chores too, so I decided to try it without the cigarette. I took a breathing break. I walked aimlessly around outside, taking in big breaths of air. It felt great, although I know I looked weird. She looked sophisticated—I looked like I was loitering.

Take at least three breathing breaks a day.

STRETCH: **Creating Sexual Energy**

This is a Stretch that many of you will look at and think, "I don't need to do this one." Throughout this book I'm going to ask you to do things that might seem stupid, weird, or scary. The process of coming out is not always comfortable, and this is one Stretch that might seem very uncomfortable. But try it anyway.

This Stretch will give you a direct experience of feeling your sexual energy as a tangible thing inside you. You will be able to create that energy and direct it. And if you can direct it within yourself, then later, in Step 3, you will be able to direct it out to others.

To some of you, the following might seem familiar. It's an old, tried-and-true tantric yoga exercise.

Masturbate and stop right *before* you orgasm. You may think it will be frustrating, but it isn't. You will feel energy in your genitals. Focus on moving the energy up to your heart. You don't have to do anything other than imagine the energy rushing upward. If you try this many times, you will find that this exercise doesn't make you horny; it makes you feel powerful and more aware of yourself as a sexual person. This exercise puts you in control of your sexuality. Many people who practice it find that it deepens their sexual experience with another. Especially if you find that orgasm depletes you, practicing this form of tantric sex will build up your endurance before orgasm and allow you to turn sex into a form of sharing. It will give you a direct, powerful experience of owning and directing your energy without giving it away.

STRETCH: **Date Yourself**

How about treating your body the way you want others to treat it? How can others love your body if you don't? Sometimes I'm so down on my body that I'm in an S&M relationship with just myself: "You big, fat, worthless piece of flesh! Down on your knees!"

Now here comes the real Stretch: try dating yourself. Make a date with yourself in advance, the way you would do with a lover. Get yourself flowers. Take yourself out to dinner and a movie. Hey, I don't put out without dinner and a movie

Artist: Ann Glover © Judy Carter

first—why should you be cheap with yourself? Then take a romantic walk with yourself on the beach. What's the matter? Are you bored with your own company? Don't be bored—talk about your date, talk about your feelings. In fact, talk about anything that truly interests you. Let yourself get turned on by the wisdom you find inside yourself.

Go home. Put on music that you really enjoy. Did you clean the house for yourself, or do you do that just for another? Remember, this is about respecting yourself. Come home and note something wonderful about your house. Remember also that this is a date and you want to get laid, so be flattering. Light some candles. Lure yourself into the bedroom. I hope you changed the sheets. Now slowly take your clothes off. Guys, this is not going to be a whip-it-out kind of evening, and girls, keep the vibrator in the drawer because it's going to be a while before you go the whole way. Really make love to yourself. Slowly, lovingly caress your body. Touch yourself all over the way you want to be touched. Don't neglect the parts of your body that don't usually get touched—your sides, feet, hands, chest. Look in the mirror and talk to yourself: "What a nice ass you have . . ." "I could go for someone like you . . ." "Wow, you must work out . . ."

Now you can go all the way, or you can just be friends, but after it's all over, don't just fall asleep on yourself.

JOURNAL WORKSHOP: Who Are You?

1. **Write in your coming-out journal what it was like to spend time with yourself.**

2. **Write a wish list of all the qualities you find attractive in another person, both personality traits and sexual turn-ons.**

3. **Now write a list of your own qualities that you take satisfaction in and those you think others find attractive in you.**

4. **Look over the list of what you want in a lover. How many of the qualities you are looking for are right inside you? If you want someone generous, loving, and loyal, do you possess those qualities? When I'm feeling insecure and critical about myself, I wouldn't want to go to bed with me. If you really want to attract a beautiful, sensual, passionate lover, become the lover you want to attract.**

Recognize also that different people are attracted to all different things and that those qualities you have—even those you may find negative—are going to be a turn-on to someone else. I know it's hard to believe, but that pot belly of yours can be a turn-on to the right person. (That's why Big Bertha invented chubby chasers.) It's a matter of matching up lists. So rather than spending time trying to shape yourself into something you imagine someone is looking for, be true to yourself in your individuality, just as you are true to yourself in your sexual orientation. And let's find that person on your wish list.

Step 3: Find Another Homo

Check those statements which are *true.*

Gays are never found . . .

❏ **in line for the Mormon Tabernacle tour**

❏ **at the Young Republican Baptists' fund-raising picnic**

❏ **knocking on your door to give you the *Watchtower***

❏ **watching reruns of *Three's Company***

❏ **listening to *Marie Osmond's Greatest Hits* album**

❏ **milking cows in Nebraska**

❏ **donating to Jesse Helms's re-election campaign**

❏ **playing football in the National Football League**

Results. If you've checked any of the above—BUZZ, you lose. Gays are everywhere. Homos are Mel

White, who for years wrote Jerry Falwell's speeches. Gays are Jean O'Leary, a well-known gay activist who was a nun. Gays are Dave Kopay, who played football for the New York Jets.

You can find a homo by driving two hours out of your small hometown to go to a gay bar, or you can save yourself time and gas money by just looking around in your own neighborhood, because there are gays where you live, work, eat, and play. As a survey once found, one out of ten individuals has experienced sex with someone of the same sex. Trying to figure out who they are can be a lot of fun. So go outside and count one, two, three, four, five, six, seven, eight, nine, gay! This could definitely make standing in line at the bank more fun.

"I read that only one percent of this country is gay. If that's true . . . I've slept with every one!"
—GAY COMIC JASON STUART

I think it's harder identifying gay women than men. Society teaches men that affection is to be exchanged with women, and a pat on the tush of another guy is okay only if you've got a number on your chest and a ball in your hand—a football. If a man looks at another man for more than a moment, straight men will look away, run away, or feel uncomfortable. So if a man holds another man's glance, chances are he's gay. But a woman can kiss another woman or even cuddle with her in bed and she's still straight!

In real life people don't give themselves away that easily. Many straights would like to think that gay people have horns or some such physical marking that makes us stand out, while in fact, we come in all shapes and sizes and dress in all different ways, which makes it hard to really be sure who's queer. Actually, it's difficult only for straights; gays seem to be able to spot other gays. Why? Because they have *gaydar*.

WHAT IS GAYDAR?

Gaydar is the ability to identify members of the tribe by picking up on their energy. Sure, it's easy to tell if someone is gay if you are in a gay bar, but what about the cute guy in your literature class at college, or that magnificent woman buying WD-40 at the hardware store? Good gaydar is the difference between wishing and knowing. Some people are blessed with great gaydar, some of us have to develop it, and some don't have a clue. "k. d. lang's gay? *Really?!*" "Oh no, you mean Liberace was gay?!"

Gaydar works like radar. The source (you) sends out a signal, and the way it bounces off the targeted object allows you to determine sexual orientation.

It may take a while to adjust your signal. When you first come out, you might have an overactive gaydar. When I realized I was gay, I wanted everyone to be gay too, which led to a lot of wishful thinking.

"Helen Hunt is gay!" Dream on, girl!

The longer you are out and the more accepting of it you are, the more refined your gaydar will be-

come. When I first started using my gaydar, I sent out a low signal because it was scary. I was afraid another woman would pick up on it, and then what? I was so frightened that the gaydar signals others sent out bounced off me as if I were a Stealth lesbian. Mostly I depended on observing obvious physical stuff to know if someone was gay, such as a gay T-shirt (one that reads, "I can't even *think* straight!" is a dead giveaway). A very short haircut on a woman who carries an excessive amount of keys can also—but not necessarily—be a clue. Or I would listen to others' language for those giveaway clues, such as "my lover," or excessive pronouns, as in, "Last night I went with *them* to the market." "Them"? Did she go with a group, or were "they" really a *she*? I mean, it is the difference between being a slut and being a lesbian.

As my gaydar improved, I stopped looking away when someone caught my eye. I started opening myself to another person's sexual energy instead of running away from it. I started registering on their screens. Beep! Beep! Beep! Gaydar . . . don't leave home without it.

STRETCH: **Tuning in to Your Gaydar**
Scoring is 1 to 10: 1 = straight, 10 = sure thing. (Bring a calculator; tabulations can be complicated.)

Find a Dyke

Okay, girls, go somewhere. Anywhere. Get out of the house and go someplace where there are people. Let's say you're in a movie line, for example.

- You see two girls together, so register it as a +1. Dyke potential. But it may be wishful thinking.

- What are they wearing? Dress and panty hose? That's a −2, but then they both could be femmes.

- Backpack +2

- Vinyl purse −1

- Political button on the purse +2

- Stiletto heels −3

- Birkenstocks +3

- But wait. What kind of movie is it? Arnold Schwarzenegger! −3

- *Go Fish* +3

- But . . . who pays? If they pay separately, −1 or +1. Could be working on codependency issues.

- If you still aren't sure, then follow them to their car. Separate cars −2. Same car +2

- Bumper stickers says, "Sappho was a right-on woman." *Major bingo! You're on the tail of a dyke!*

But now try it using advanced gaydar, depending less on physical evidence and more on instinct. For example:

- I'm grocery shopping and I look at this beautiful woman, and she meets my eye. +1

- She holds the look for more than three seconds. +3

- Her nipples get hard in her leotard. +2

- Then I realize we're in the frozen food section. −1

- But she takes off her jacket anyway. +3

- She follows me to check out and seems to be checking out more than food. +2

- She picks up *McCall's* magazine. −3

- She turns to the article on Melissa Etheridge. +3

- I brush my arm against hers and she sighs. +3

- I look at her and say, "Let's go." She's says, "Anywhere." +500

Find a Fag

Boys, try this. You're at a mall and you see a cute guy.

- **You look at each other, +1; but then he glances away, –1.**
- **You both walk away. –2**
- **But then you both turn around and look back at each other at the same time. +2**
- **He changes his direction and follows you. +4**
- **But then he walks into Sears. –3**
- **You follow him in and he's buying tires for his Jeep. +3**
- **He looks at you and you notice that his tires are not the only thing that *is* steel belted. It's a +10.**

Okay, so all signals are "go" on your gaydar. Now what do you do? Come out.

HANGING WITH THE HOMIES

The problem is you don't want straight people to know you're gay, because you're not out, but you do want other gay people to know, so you can get laid. So you walk the narrow pink line because in order to get laid, you need to come out, at least a little.

If you are unwilling to be out, the safest way to find gay people without outing yourself is to go to places that *only* homos go: gay bars, gay festivals, the Liberace mausoleum. There we can feel comfortable being who we are, away from the hostile glances of homophobes. These are safe places to out ourselves because everyone is there for the same reason. We gays now also have our very own newspapers, dances, festivals, expos, on-line electronic networks, political organizations, theaters, twelve-step programs, Olympics, ski clubs, social groups within the workplace, TV shows, and vacation spots.

Fortunately, as more and more gay people feel comfortable in coming out, the culture as a whole benefits by becoming socially more well rounded. For many years, gay bars were the only place where gay people could gather publicly and feel at ease. Now we can feel more comfortable within mixed, hetero-and-homo groups.

"If you removed all of the homosexuals and homosexual influence from what is generally regarded as American culture, you would be pretty much left with *Let's Make a Deal*."
—WRITER FRAN LEBOWITZ

Being in our own places, where everyone is gay, it's easier to let go. In those environments, many of us change the way we walk, talk, and dress. It's amazing how, when Friday comes, men trade in their suits for tight jeans and women take off their panty hose and strut down Christopher Street in New York's Greenwich Village. Come the weekend, you can feel the energy flow down Santa Monica Boulevard in West Hollywood as people take to the streets shedding their fake, hetero personas.

GAY BARS

Nobody ever forgets the first time they walked into a gay bar. It's so exciting. "Everybody here is gay!" It's like going to Mecca. It's the Homo Shopping Network of love.

So Many Bars, So Little Time

There are publications, such as the *Gay Yellow Pages*, that have listings of bars. Many of the trendier clubs are transient in nature, and locations are constantly changing, so it would be wise to call first before you go anywhere. Call information and get the number of anything gay and lesbian, and don't pretend to be doing it for a friend. Go ahead, out yourself to the information operator—chances are you're never going to meet that person, and so what if you did?

If you are too shy to call information, look in the yellow pages under

"I could just die! I've been cruising the man who flunked me in seventh-grade English!"

"Social Organizations." There should be listings there of gay groups. It is best to get some advice about the best bars for you to go to, lest you go out because you feel like dancing and end up in a sex club.

Depending on how far out in the sticks you live, there's bound to be a gay bar within fifteen miles. Okay, fifty miles, if you live in the Yukon Territory, but remember, they don't call it *Klondike* for nothing. Gay bars come in all varieties:

- **Country Western—Can be both very friendly and sexually unintimidating. Most have dance lessons on certain nights. It's a beer-drinking, foot-stomping crowd. A lot of couples and singles, usually a mixture of both gays and lesbians. People ask one another to dance, and my experience is that there is less attitude to be found here than at some other clubs. This may not be your mug of beer, but it can make for a fun evening.**

- **Large Disco Bars—Sometimes these have lofts and multiple floors, each with its own attitude. Looks and dress are what count if you want to get noticed. Attire is tight and trendy. Not much conversation; communication is mostly physical.**

- **Neighborhood Gay Bars— The activity is mostly conversation, drinking, and pool. More intimate and friendly. A place where you can be yourself while you meet your neighbors. Neighborhood bars seem to have either a young crowd or an older crowd. A good place for young men to find "Daddy"!**

- **Sex Clubs—Private memberships. Sometimes no beds, no rooms, just a sweaty garage where men drop their pants**

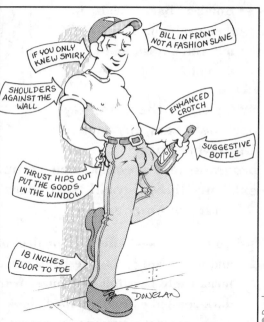

The Bar Pose. In a good spot under indirect lighting (according to age), place shoulder flat against a wall or post. Thrust hips forward and, if you "dress" on the left, your left foot must be placed exactly 18 inches from the floor against the wall. This raises the thigh, displaying your basket to maximum effect. A long-neck beer bottle (it's so butch), gripped suggestively, should rest on the raised thigh. Your expression should be slightly amused and slightly bored. Never smile until you're reeling him in.

and do whatever men do when they drop their pants. I wouldn't know any more, and I try not to think much about it! It's a club, kind of like the NRA, but different. No names or intimacy required here. BYOG—bring your own genitals.

- Bathhouse—Same as a sex club, but with rooms and yards of terry cloth.

- Bondage Bars—Cruise it, then bruise it. Also BYOG, but with a twist, and I mean it.

"Hold it, pal . . . Do you know you're doing forty in a twenty-five-year-old zone?"

Artist: Donelan © Judy Carter

"Why aren't there any gay-nerd-bear bars, anyway? Ones where bear programmers network their computers through glory holes and exchange filthy E-mail? Now, there's a market!"
—WRITER ANTHONY BERNO

- Coffeehouses—Caffeine. Nonalcoholic places to talk, read the paper, and meet. Not just for lesbians anymore as gay people look for an alternative to bars full of drunks. Warning! After two or three hours of dark-roasted caffeine, nobody looks good. But if you're looking for company, pick someone 'cause you're not sleeping tonight anyway.

WARNING ABOUT LOOKING FOR RELATIONSHIPS IN BARS

If you're just looking to get laid, a gay bar is the place to be. Be aware that the qualities that work well in a bar aren't necessarily the qualities that work in life. Bars are mostly about superficial things, namely looks, looks, looks, and attitude. Looks and youth go far in a bar. Given the qualities of what people look for in a bar, a guy like Jeffrey Dahmer can score and an Albert Einstein will go home alone. When people go out to get laid, those Madison Avenue stereotypes come into play.

If your goal is to get into a relationship, you might want to try meeting someone in places other than bars. A good way to meet people likely to be compatible is while you're doing the things that you like to do. When you're being yourself, doing things you enjoy doing, you are more likely to meet others who share your interests. It's not guaranteed, however. I met a beautiful woman on a hike. I took for granted that she, like me, was an outdoorsy type, not knowing that this was the first hike she had taken in ten years. Our relationship lasted only slightly longer than the hike. Maybe the relationship would have worked out if I'd met her doing the activity she enjoyed doing most—napping.

Be true to yourself and meet others doing things you enjoy. And if there's nothing you like to do, then you don't need a lover—you need a life.

TEST: WHAT DO YOU LIKE?

❏ skiing	❏ eating (food)	❏ other:
❏ bicycling	❏ dancing	_____
❏ scuba diving	❏ stamp collecting	_____
❏ hiking	❏ comedy	_____
❏ reading	❏ animals	_____
❏ movies	❏ computers	_____

PLACES TO MEET OTHER HOMOS

For everything you've checked, there is a gay group—yes, even for gay stamp collectors. If you are a skier, in L.A. alone there are two gay ski groups. There is also National Gay Ski Week in Aspen, Colorado, and at Whistler in Canada. Scuba diving has the National Diving for Life, an annual weeklong dive whose proceeds go to gay charities. There are the gay and lesbian chapters of the Sierra Club, gay rodeos, gay churches, gay comedy nights, gay movie clubs, gay book clubs, gay restaurant-dining clubs. I walk my dogs each week with a lesbian dog-walking club—and some of the *women* are lesbians too!

If you've added something to my list above, there may well be a club for that too. If not, you could start one. Chances are there are other people out there who share your interest, unless you're into something as obscure as, say, naked bingo because you get off anytime you hear the phrase *O-69.* Look in the Appendix for the organization near you. You don't need to do it alone.

"Empowerment seminar? . . . Please. I'm a bull dyke, you don't get more empowered than this."

College Classes

A great way to meet other gays is at your local community college. If you see a class called Gender Issues in America, take it. Chances are you'll meet someone.

Get Political

Get involved with one of the hundreds of gay rights groups and give service (political service!) while you meet others.

Gays and lesbians do things differently.

Get On-Line

Get out of emergency parking and on the superhighway of love. Whether you are looking for love, sex, or Big Bertha, you're sure to find it on-line. You can anonymously connect to people all across the world. America Online features a very complete and active Gay and Lesbian Community Forum. Anyone with a modem can gab on a variety of topics. As of the writing this book, here are some of the topics in the Gay and Lesbian Community Forum on America Online:

Gay Message Board for Men	*Lesbian Message Board*
• **bears**	• **women of leather**
• **military gays**	• **butch/femme talk**
• **gay coparenting**	• **lesbian erotica**
• **teen gays**	• **coming-out stories**
• **gay Russians**	• **menopause**
• **gay cigar lovers**	• **falling for a hetero**
• **gay Germans**	• **interracial relations**
• **gay American Indians**	• **two-step dykes**
• **gay Disney fans**	• **twelve-stepping dykes**
• **surviving the loss of a partner**	• **camping lesbians**
• **big men**	• **dykes with pets**
• **gay and Jewish**	• **baby dykes**
• **gay Italians**	• **nice Jewish girls**
• **black and gay**	• **lesbians hurting lesbians**
• **college gays**	• **rural lesbians**
• **fifty-plus gays**	• **couples issues**

There's also *hot-chatting*, where you can meet someone special, take them to a private room, and hot-chat. Ladies, careful about who you are hot-chatting with. "Hot Bi Momma" might turn out to be a geeky eighteen-year-old guy named Milton; straight teenaged boys seem to get off on this. Before hot-chatting, ask him a question that only another lesbian would know. If he says his clitoris is eight inches long, chances are you're chatting with an impostor.

If you want any information about anything gay, hook into the Queer Resource Directory on the Internet. This is an electronic library with news clippings, political-contact information, newsletters, essays, images, and every other kind of information resource of interest to the gay community. The electronic library is available to anyone who has a modem and access to the Internet.

Another way to get information is to get on electronic mailing lists. By subscribing to any of the hundreds of groups, you can have information come directly to you via E-mail. You can receive free-of-charge updates from gay and lesbian groups such as Action Alert, National Organization of Gay and Lesbian Scientists and Technical Professionals, Metropolitan Community Church Family in Christ, and local updates from groups such as Amarillo Lesbian/Gay Alliance. Exciting! Check out the Appendix of this book for a resource of E-mail mailing lists.

Gay Bookstores

Virtually every city with a substantial gay population has a gay bookstore. Not to be mistaken for the sleazy porno stores with sticky floors, flickering fluorescent lights and a clerk that has a just-got-out-of-jail stubble and a permanent line of drool at the corner of his mouth. The bookstores I'm talking about are respectable gay and lesbian establishments that have become cornerstones in the gay community. They are safe places to get information regarding upcoming events, purchase tickets, books, magazines, postcards, greeting cards, and network with people who share the same interests.

Gay Neighborhoods

You can feel totally comfortable kissing on your front porch by living in a gay neighborhood. How do you know when you're in the gay part of town? If . . .

- **the houses are tasteful and newly remodeled**

- **the local movie theater has films with dialogue**

- **the deli has items other than Velveeta and pimento loaf**

- **there are a lot of Jeep Cherokees in the driveways**

"No. We tried separate vacations last year and he *had way too much fun."*

- **brunch is served any time of the day**
- **the local watering hole is called Boys "R" Us**
- **the coffee shops make cappuccinos with coffee other than Yuban**

. . . then you are there.

Or you can find a gay real estate agent to assist you. Look through the ads in your local gay newspaper.

Gay Vacation Places

Want to kiss your lover along a romantic stretch of beach? Go on a vacation with gay people, or go to Gay Club Med, Key West, Provincetown, RSVP Cruises, or Olivia Cruises, or take advantage of any number of other vacation possibilities geared to gays. It's a vacation—be yourself!

Gay Magazines

Subscribe to a gay magazine. They usually arrive in a plain manila envelope, so you won't get outed to your letter carrier. For a listing of gay publications, check out the Appendix.

STRETCH: Do Research

If you really wanted, chances are you could be at a gay event every day of the week. Find out what gay resources are offered in your neck of the woods. Check out all the avenues listed above.

Write down what is available to you and what interests you. If there is nothing in your neighborhood, then check out how far away the closest gay bar or event is. If you determine that there simply is nothing close enough to you to be practical, then you may want to consider a move. It's not by accident there are so many homos in places like New York, Atlanta, Los Angeles, Houston, San Francisco, Chicago, and Washington, D.C. They weren't all born there, you know.

Places I could go to meet gays:

Place   *Phone/address*

_____

_____

_____

_____

OUT YOURSELF TO ANOTHER HOMO

Do you never get hit on? Are you never a bleep on someone's gaydar? Are you a Stealth homo?

Okay, to get laid, you are going to have to out yourself. It's easy if you are in a gay bar, where it's assumed that everyone is there for the same reason. But many, many times we find ourselves attracted to someone we just aren't sure about. We may even have gone out with them, and it's still not clear if we are on a date or just friends. It's agony looking for clues. You think they're gay, but you don't fully trust your gaydar.

"Pâté?"

FAIL-SAFE WAYS TO OUT YOURSELF

- If you say, "I heard about this interesting movie, *The Amazing Adventure of Two Girls in Love.* Have you heard of it?" and they say, "I was first in line the day it opened," DYKE!

- "Where do you go for fun around here?" If they mention Hooters, then STRAIGHT! Unless they're a woman, and then BUTCH!

- If you say, "Did you see the guy on *Oprah* who came out to his family on national TV? That must have been really hard. What do you think about that?" and they say, "That was very courageous and I sent a copy to my parents," GAY! And if they say, "Came out? What do you mean? Where was he going?" STRAIGHT and STUPID!

GAY ACCESSORIES

Another way to out yourself is to use gay accessories. Remember, the first step in selling a house is to put a sign out front.

Try wearing freedom rings or pink triangles and let other gays know who you are. And feel safe because heteros don't have a clue what you're getting at. Why should they? Heteros are way too self-obsessed with their own dramas to pay any attention to our underground symbols.

I was at a store wearing my freedom-ring necklace, which looks something like Fruit Loops on a string. There were two people behind the counter, and one of them said to me, "I like your necklace." It was his way of safely identifying himself as a member of my tribe without outing himself to his boss. We exchanged smiles and once again acknowledged that we are everywhere.

"I'm afraid, sister, that we are going to ask you to return to the traditional habit."

TEST: HOW OUT ARE YOU?

Here are some T-shirt titles from *Don't Panic,* a T-shirt company that carries gay-oriented merchandise. Circle which T-shirts you would be willing to wear in public.

The daring of the T-shirt you wear is a litmus test of just how out you are. It's one thing to wear your "I can't even *think* straight" T-shirt when strolling with your lover, but are you still willing to wear it to the auto repair shop?

Artist: Ann Glover © Don't Panic TShirts

GET YOUR GAY IDENTITY TOGETHER

The best part about being out is the freedom from the restraints of gender dressing. I'll never forget the initial confusion of dressing to go out on a date with another woman. Most of my life to that point I had dressed to please a man, wearing not what I wanted, but what I thought he would want. My mother, who owned a Beverly Hills dress store we all affectionately referred to as Jews for Polyester, was obsessed with having me wear the right clothing. "Judy, that's not what *they're* wearing." I never met "them," but I knew I had to please

"them," and "they" were always right and I was always wrong. I wore heels although they put my back out, and no matter how hard I tried, I always walked like a dyke in them. Going out with another woman made me think of what I'd enjoy seeing on a woman. What do I like? Since I'd been brought up programmed to please, that thought was a first.

The world opened up to me with the new thought of dressing to please myself and not dressing to adapt to current fashion. There is tremendous pressure to conform, pressure coming from all sides, straight and gay. It's so limiting, especially since my Rubenesque body has been out of style since 1898. What freedom it is to dress in a way that's comfortable to my sensibilities! They say that gentlemen prefer Hanes, and I say that's great—because they sure don't fit women! Where are my Doc Martens?

The incredible thing is that gay fashion and gender-bending clothes have emerged as the new style. It's strange that many heteros don't want to be associated with us, but they sure like to dress like us. The heteros have adopted our styles now, as straight men wear jeans with tears in the ass and pierce their ears (and other body parts) for earrings, and straight girls wear hiking boots. It's getting hard to tell who the gays are. We gays have always been trendsetters, and it all comes from daring to be different. Hey, it wasn't Annie Hall who started women wearing ties, but a butch dyke in New Jersey named Doris.

Cleaning out your closets is not only a metaphor but a wonderful way for you to let go of unnecessary items that are clogging your life.

Jock Dyke
Never seen in street clothes.

S&M Lesbian
"Down on your knees, Martha!"

Lipstick Lesbian
"Ding-dong, Avon calling."

Preppie Lesbian
Learned golf at Smith College.

Earth Momma Lesbian
Seen at music festivals with tube pasta dish.

Butch Dyke
Packin' Snap-on tools.

Artist: Donelan © Judy Carter

Different Types of Lesbians

Go in your closet and throw away everything you haven't worn in the last year. Get rid of it, give it away, donate it, sell it. Just like your old fears, these clothes aren't yours any-more, and, thank Big Bertha, they're not mine.

You might think that this

EVERY TIME I GET SO DEPRESSED THAT I DON'T KNOW WHERE I AM, I GO TO A SHOPPING MALL AND STAND IN FRONT OF THE STORE DIRECTORY BECAUSE IT SAYS: "YOU ARE HERE."

Artist: Ann Glover © Judy Carter

is a stretch you can pass over. If you do you will be missing a very important part of the coming-out process. We are all carrying around old baggage, and for some of us those bags are full of bad clothes. Get rid of those bell-bottoms and mohair jackets, those pants you'll fit into when you lose that weight. Be here now, and get rid of the junk of your past. Go do it now! You'll end up with an empty closet. Then, time to go shopping!

If you wore exactly what you want to wear without regard to current fashion, what would you like to be wearing now? (Buzz cut, nipple ring . . .) Write three items here:

1. _____

2. _____

3. _____

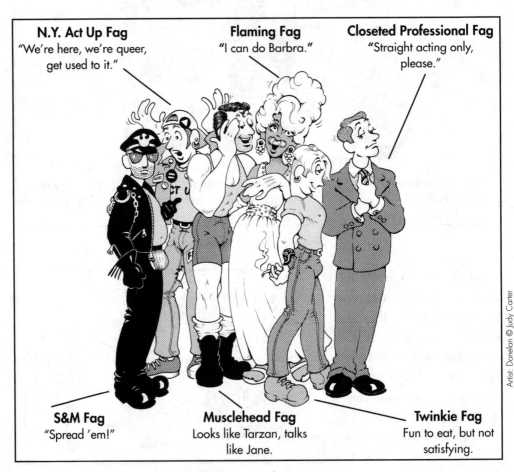

Different Types of Gay Men

Artist: Donelan © Judy Carter

"It's hard losing weight when you're a lipstick lesbian. It's hard eating Jenny Craig when you've got Mary Kay on your face."
—ANONYMOUS

THE PERSONALS AD—COMING OUT IN TWENTY WORDS OR LESS

It amazes me how people will spend so much energy moaning about not meeting anyone new and yet not do anything about it. With the same energy you spend complaining, you could be advertising. Don't keep yourself the best-kept secret around.

" 'I'm new to the gay scene.' Boy, that works with gay men. I've been using that in my personal ad for the last ten years now."
—GAY COMIC MICHAEL RASKY

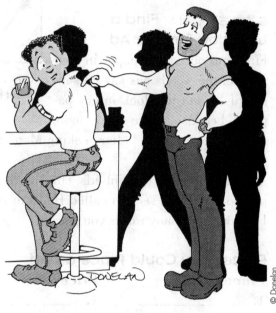

"You. Twenty-five words or less . . . why should you be my next lover?"

There are two ways of finding a like-oriented person using personals ads. One is to respond to an ad and the other is to create one for yourself. Creating one for yourself is the more powerful way to meet someone. It puts you in control of getting out the word on exactly what you want.

Writing a personals ad can be better than therapy, and at twenty-five cents a word, it's a lot cheaper. You have to decide how you can best represent yourself with a limited amount of words.

- **What is the most important thing about you?**

- **What do you want? Romance, friends, dating, sex—what?**

- **What don't you want? "No smokers, drinkers, serial killers, or curiosity seekers."**

- **What do you enjoy doing? Skiing, drinking, eating, sleeping—what?**

But be careful what you ask for—you might get it. You might ask for someone who is so perfect—*no* smoking, *no* drinking, *no* problems—and end up with someone who is *no* fun. Would you mind someone who was great in bed and smoked a little, or some churchgoing anal retentive who has stripped themselves of all shortcomings?

"Sure . . . it said 'watersports and old movies' . . . but he showed up in Esther Williams drag."

STRETCH: Find a Location for Your Ad

First find out which paper in your neck of the woods has gay personals ads. Don't just look in gay papers, because more and more straight papers have "Men Seeking Men" and "Women Seeking Women" personals.

Don't just stick to print ads. On America Online there is a way to post your personals ad in a section called Heart to Heart in the gay and lesbian boards. Find out how many words you get.

Places You Could Place an Ad

Place	*Price*	*Number of Words*
1. _____	1. _____	1. _____
2. _____	2. _____	2. _____
3. _____	3. _____	3. _____
4. _____	4. _____	4. _____
5. _____	5. _____	5. _____

Take five minutes and circle how many words describe you.

You are:

GWM, gay white man

GBM, gay black man

GLM, gay Latin man

GJM, gay Jewish man

GWF

GBF

GJF

attractive

thin

well-built

gorgeous

hunk

sweet

soft

sensitive

soft-butch

ultrafemme

bi—curious

femme

gallant butch

dominant top

submissive

down-to-earth

cute

nonbutch

cocoa skinned

feminine

full figured

lovable

exotic

full-figured beauty

feminine to soft butch

androg/fem

well endowed

funny

lipstick lesbian

spiritual

tough looking but big

passionate

hearted

lighthearted

fun

stable

doesn't play games

conservative, str8-act-
ing

professional, mature

imaginative

hairy

okay looking

good personality

HIV–

HIV+

military man

serious

open minded

exotic

professional

interestingly
attractive

chubby

masculine

hirsute

smooth body

muscular

surfer type

totally unique

adorable

Continued

PERSONALS ADS
STARTER KIT

YOU ARE:

SEEKS:

I WANT: _____

IF YOU
WRITE IT,
THEY WILL
COME

cutting-edge	**Middle Eastern**	artist
sincere	**European**	tomboy
police officer	**professional**	age _____
traditional	**Chicano**	occupation _____
sophisticated	**Chinese**	hobby _____
ready for	**Cuban**	twelve-step
relationship	**Italian**	program _____
wholesome	**Japanese**	other _____
discreet with	**Jewish**	other _____
integrity	**cop**	other _____
no games	**ex-cop**	other _____
petite femme	**not into bar scene**	other _____
boyish gam	**fun loving**	other _____
buddy type	**confidant**	other _____
college guy	**financially responsible**	

Latino

Now circle what you want. Circle what you *really* want, not what you think you're supposed to have. You might *think* you want a responsible, steady job, to be rich and end up with Janet Reno. Circle what would really turn you on, and do it quickly without thinking.

I'm seeking:

age _____	soft butch	friend
race _____	ultrafemme	lover
passionate	femme	skier
attractive	gallant butch	well endowed
thin	life soul mate	scuba diver
gorgeous	dominant top	lovable
hunk	submissive	full-figured beauty
sweet	down-to-earth	feminine to soft
soft	cute	butch
sensitive	nonbutch	*Continued*

androg/fem

funny

lipstick lesbian

spiritual

tough looking

big hearted

nurturing

stable

doesn't play games

conservative, str8-
    acting

professional, mature

imaginative

hairy

HIV–

HIV+

military man

bayou boy

very good looking

serious only

open minded

monogamist

exotic

rich

financially stable

interestingly
    attractive

masculine

hirsute

smooth body

muscular

surfer type

totally unique

adorable

cutting-edge

sincere

race unimportant

adven2rus, cr8iv

police officer

tradition and
    sophistication

available

wholesome

discreet with integrity

no games

GWM boyish gam

buddy type

college guy

very discreet

Latino

Middle Eastern

European

professional

Chicano

Chinese

Cuban

Italian

chubby

Japanese

Jewish

cop

ex-cop

not into bar scene

fun loving

travel companion

confidant

financially
    responsible

moody, rogue/artist

tomboy

smoker

nonsmoker

other _____

other _____

other _____

other _____

other _____

other _____

other _____

Continued

Now, circle what you want to do with them.

I want:

sex	romantic dinners	quiet eves at home
beach walks	game	noisy eves out
seder	dating	eating out
Scrabble	skiing	traveling
Boggle	scuba diving	let's have coffee
nude pictures	muff diving	first romance possible
lake walks	companionship	
desert walks	friendship	dancing and romancing
hiking	relationship	other _____
laughs	fly-fishing	other _____
church	talking	other _____
fun times and possibly more	working out	other _____
nurturing	adventures	other _____

WRITING THE AD

....

Put these lists away for a few days and give yourself time for other things to come to mind that you want to include. Then each morning write them down. When you think you've covered all your bases, look over the list and put a star next to the words that stand out. What you see may surprise you. Some people start out thinking they just want sex, but their ad reveals that what they really want is companionship, maybe even just someone to go to the movies with them—and then get laid afterwards.

Using these starred words, put together your personals ad. And while you're at it, get your priorities straight about what you want. For example, is a sense of humor more important than no smoking? After all, someone can give up smoking, but do you really want to spend the rest of your life listening to knock-knock jokes? Play with the words. Vary the order. You might want to put each word on a separate piece of paper and arrange them that way. Try to have fun with it and remember to be honest with yourself.

Okay, so are you going to keep yourself a secret, or are you willing to put what you want out there? Whether or not you meet Ms. or Mr. Right from the personals ad, just putting it out can have an amazing effect. Let me tell you my own story . . .

I hadn't been with someone for a year, and I decided to place my first personals ad. It was hard describing myself, and scary admitting what I wanted. After a week of writing, I scaled the ad down from essay size to something affordable and called it in to the paper. I was shaking. It was like some phase of a twelve-step program, one in which I had to admit to this stranger at the other end of the phone my heart's desire. I was scared that she would laugh or even recognize my voice: "Is this Judy Carter?" Although my name

"Exactly what did you put in your ad?"

and phone number were not in the ad, she asked for the name on the credit card and my phone number for their confidential records. It felt as if my ovums were on the line. This was like talking to Big Bertha.

The next day I met my lover, although the ad didn't come out until the day *after* I met her. Just the act of writing down what I wanted, admitting it to another person, and sending it out into the universe made it become very real.

So call, fax, mail, or E-mail your ad into a paper. Do it today. Then clean up your house because someone's coming over.

ANSWERING PERSONALS ADS

When reading personals ads, read between the lines; virtually nothing is as it seems. It's like the real estate ads. When they describe a house, *charming* means small, *spacious* means no walls, *quaint* means falling apart. It's not so much what they say it's what they don't say.

In answering an ad, you might be asked to send a photo. The ad might claim that the other person has a "a body that would stop a clock." When you meet them you might realize that their body might stop a clock—but only if they sat on it.

> **"'Well endowed?' Where do you measure? From the small of your back?"**
> —GAY COMIC ANT

If you do send a photo, it's probably best to send one of just you and not one of you and your ex kissing in bed, even if it had been a good hair day. And in return, you can and should ask them for a picture, a recent picture. People tend to change a lot from their senior year in high school, and not always for the better.

Then sometimes a phone number is given, and you may be asked to call. If you do meet the other

"Just a bunch of bills for dad and me . . . and a letter addressed to. . . . 'Helium Heels'?"

person over the phone, ask him or her a lot of questions and really listen to what that person has to say. If you like what you hear and want to make plans to get together, make it a short meeting, something like an afternoon coffee. Keep it brief, and never let anyone know where you live until you are as sure as possible that you're not dealing with an ax murderer.

Remember, when placing a personal ad . . .

1. **Be honest about yourself (but don't put yourself down): "Worthless piece of shit seeking same."**

2. **Be as precise as possible in describing just what it is you are looking for: "GWF graphic designer who loves springer spaniels, tapioca pudding with lumps, traveling to Kenya, scuba driving in 82-degree water, seeks whatever."**

3. **Be realistic: "Unemployed, aging, fat GM seeks financially secure surfer dude."**

4. **Just remember to follow through, but go slowly and be patient. Bed partners are everywhere, but finding the right person to spend the rest of your life with, or even just a weekend with, is probably going to take a little time. Let's face it, it's easy to find someone to take you to bed. It's harder to find someone to take you to the airport.**

WARNING—RED FLAG: If you hear a potential date say any of the following—throw down the red flag.

- "My surgeon says that my breasts are almost finished."

- "Let's meet at a place I'm familiar with . . . the park."

- "The weight is really coming off."

- "I can meet you at 2 P.M. after my appointment at the methadone clinic."

- "I can fit you in for an hour in between my codependency meeting, Al-Anon meeting, my Shoplifters, Thieves Anonymous meeting, and my sex addicts meeting."

- "Is where you want to meet near a bus line?"

- "Is the coffee there expensive?"

- "Anytime is good. I'm between jobs."

- "Let me check with my probation officer."

- "Oh, that time wouldn't be good. That's when my lover's home."

- "That restaurant sounds good. Are you sure they have a bar there?"

- "Come over on Tuesday. My parents won't be home then."

But if getting laid is what you want . . . read on.

Step 4: Get Laid

Check what applies.

Women

❑ Are you keeping your fingernails short?

❑ Are you ordering needless items from catalogs just to catch a glimpse of the UPS girl?

❑ Has your *Desert Hearts* videotape broken because you've watched the sex scene too many times?

❑ Are you actually throwing away that baggy cotton underwear with holes in it?

❑ Are you macraméing plant hangers but have no plants?

❑ Are you finding yourself watching reruns of *Charlie's Angels*?

❑ Can you read *The Joy of Lesbian Sex* only with one hand?

❑ Do you find yourself suddenly wanting to ride horses?

Guys

❑ Are you awake?

If you've answered yes to any of these questions, you are ready to get laid. Whether you've done it or just dreamt it, we all want to do it better, thinner, bigger, firmer, harder, slower, louder and *more*, MORE, MORE. If you've never done it, by following the exercises in this chapter you just might be able to turn your dreams into a reality. And if you're now *doing it,* the exercises in this chapter will help make your reality dreamy!

There is no right way to get laid; there are only the consequences. Gay sex happens in all different ways, and when two people are both consenting and playing it safe, then all those ways are right. It happens between lovers, friends, and strangers. It happens at Dick Dock in P-town, in the woods at women's music festivals, and even in Tuscaloosa, Alabama. It happens with love, like, and indifference. And none of it is wrong.

"The only unnatural sexual act is that which you cannot perform."
—ALFRED KINSEY

So when we come out to our sexuality and bring it out in the open, we become more comfortable with who we are. As gays, we all deserve to have a healthy, happy sex life. Even straight people deserve that!

GAYS AND LESBIANS ARE DIFFERENT

According to my research—I interviewed over one thousand gays and lesbians—there appear to be differences when it comes to getting laid. Gay men seem to get laid, and lesbians seem to get into relationships.

"You know that joke: 'What do lesbians bring on their second date? A U-Haul.' That's a stupid joke. What do lesbians need with a U-Haul? We all have pickup trucks."
—LESBIAN COMIC LYNDA MONTGOMERY

GETTING-LAID PROCEDURE FOR MEN

STEP ONE: Get out of the house.

STEP TWO: You're laid.

Note: If you get out of the house and find yourself in the Midwest, then get to a coast—any coast—and then get out of the house. You'll get laid.

GETTING-LAID PROCEDURE FOR WOMEN

STEP ONE: Dream about it.

STEP TWO: Write about it in your journal.

STEP THREE: Talk about it in your women's study course.

STEP FOUR: Cry and hold each other as you talk about your childhood pain.

STEP FIVE: Kiss.

STEP SIX: Process the kiss in therapy.

STEP SEVEN: Discuss boundary issues.

STEP EIGHT: Cuddle.

STEP NINE: You're laid.

STEP TEN: Next day, you're living together in a committed relationship.

"It's interesting how homosexuals just live on the coast. It's as if God looks down and one day says, 'Okay, all of you homosexuals move to the side.'"

—LESBIAN COMIC GEORGIA RAGSDALE

Gay men and lesbians demonstrate totally different sexual behaviors. I researched this subject. I rented two movies. One was depicted as a love story about two gay guys, and the other was a love story about two women. The gay male video starts off with the two guys playing basketball. Thirty *seconds* into this movie, one guy looks at the other and says, "I'm sweaty,

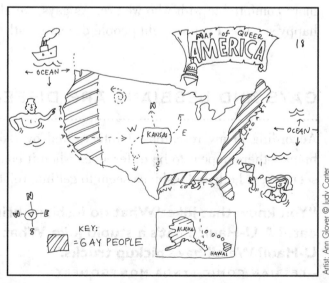

let's fuck." Obviously, in male flicks, love comes easy. Thirty *minutes* into lesbian film *Desert Hearts,* they're still shopping. We *are* different. I've seen some gay guys go out to gay bars dressed as cops. I've never been to a lesbian bar and seen anyone dressed as a meter maid. We are different.

We are different!

But when it comes to fulfilling our sexual desires, the gays and lesbians I interviewed had many similarities. Did you know that many lesbians watch gay male porno to get turned on? Did you know that many gay men watch gay male porno to get turned on? Wow! We do have a lot in common, including questions such as:

- **How do I find a lover?**
- **How do I know if they are gay without first outing myself?**
- **How do I know if someone is interested in me?**
- **How do I bring up safe sex?**
- **What's a fuck buddy and where do I find one?**

So with that in mind, let's move on to the matter at hand. Or to getting it out of a hand and into bed. (Sorry, I couldn't resist!)

BAR CRUISIN'

....

You're in a gay bar and there he/she is. Beautiful, yes! You summon up all your courage and you saunter over there. You stand right next to this incredible beauty. You give your hair a confident toss. The lust object turns and looks at you. You open your mouth and say, "I, ah, uhm, uh, well, sorry . . . bye."

Sometimes, when we are attracted to someone, English becomes a second language. It happens to everyone. Okay, it happens to me . . . a lot. That's why, when cruisin', it helps to have a line to break the ice. And just what that line will be is all-important. Obviously, there are some lines that work better than others. For the sake of variety, let's look at some bad lines first. None of these lines work—at least not when I tried them.

TOP TEN WORST PICKUP LINES

1. Don't you just hate war?

2. Excuse me, did you leave these dental dams outside?

3. Didn't I see you at a Rush Limbaugh book signing?

4. Weren't you at the free clinic last week?

5. Don't you hate dumb pickup lines?

6. Is your penis pierced? (Women don't react well to this line.)

7. God, you look like my mother. (Men don't react well to this line.)

8. Boy, these crabs are killing me.

9. I can get you on *Baywatch*.

10. What the world needs now is love, sweet love. Don't you agree?

"I just won the lottery, and. . . . Gee . . . I don't know what to do with all that money."

Actually, anything that sounds like a line won't work. And unless you're David Letterman, trying to be funny usually is a real turnoff. The best way to break the ice is to make someone else feel good about themselves in an honest, direct way, and if it happens to make them laugh, that's great too!

BEST WAYS TO BREAK THE ICE

1. Compliment them. "You're a great dancer." "I love your bracelet." "Where did you get that great watch?" "Silver looks good on you." "What a great dog collar!"

   Flirting is just as simple as showing interest in them. And isn't that what we all want? We all want attention. And the person who can give it in a positive way becomes very desirable.

2. **Share an observation.** Negative ones work the best if you think the other person will agree with you. "This place really isn't very friendly, is it?" "This music really sucks, doesn't it?"

3. **If you're not at an obviously gay place** (like a bar) or event (like a lesbian hoedown), take a risk and out yourself. "I'm just checking out my gaydar. Are you?"

4. **Just introduce yourself.** Sometimes a simple introduction like, "Hi, my name is Judy," is the best icebreaker—unless, of course, your name is Fred, in which case more than the ice might get broken. This may not establish you as the witty, clever person you want to seem, but it is clean and simple. Just an elegant act of courage, of walking up to a stranger, putting your hand out, making eye contact, and introducing yourself, can work wonderfully. You'll feel the energy start flowing and you'll feel welcome, or you'll feel no warmth at all, which could be a good sign that the person sitting next to your chosen one is a lover. Oops! So what? If she's a lesbian, in three months she'll probably break up with her and be dating you.

If you don't want to approach someone you're attracted to, you can wait for that person to come over to you. Or you can wait for someone to introduce you. Or you can wait for an earthquake to slide him or her into your lap. We all know people who invariably get what they want; we call them lucky. Hey, sure, luck happens, but it happens to people who take action. Luck happens a lot faster when you make it happen.

"Action may not always bring happiness, but there is no happiness without action."
—BENJAMIN DISRAELI

NOW THAT YOU'VE BROKEN THE ICE
....

A great line might be a good icebreaker, but nobody gets laid because they make good speeches. Face it, Abraham Lincoln was not a sexual god. He gave a mean speech, but there's no historical evidence that he was in demand under the sheets.

You really can't plan or rehearse flirting. Flirting just happens, but first you've got to feel free enough to take off your restraints. Sure, sometimes you need the assistance of a line to break the ice (or a good stiff drink could help too), but if that chemistry is really there, a reaction will occur without your having to be witty, clever, or thin.

Foreplay starts when you meet. You aren't exchanging fluids, but you are exchanging energy even before you swap phone numbers. You'll feel a rush, a quickening, a heightened sense of yourself. Don't squelch it. Go with it. Relax. This *could* be the one.

Can only one person be attracted? Not for long. Just as a log will quickly burn out without being next to another log, sexual energy will dissipate with no one there to return it. It can be dangerous if someone doesn't return the energy and you find yourself still obsessed with that person. Soon it's not about log burning but about burning down their house—see "Stalking"—and you're fast becoming a candidate for a restraining order.

WARNING: BE CAREFUL NOT TO TURN HOSTILE WHEN FLIRTING.

Try approaching someone without developing great expectations. So if you ask someone to dance and they say no, then, fine—their loss—you have nothing invested.

I used to have entire love relationships with women I had never even spoken to. I would only have to see an attractive woman across a dance floor, and before I even asked her to dance, I would be thinking of how we would make love, where we would go on our honeymoon, and what we would name our dogs. So by the time I actually walked across the floor and asked her to dance, I was already in a committed relationship. And if she said, "No thanks, I'm here with my lover," I'm already thinking, "How could you cheat on me like that? You bitch!"

STRETCH: Become a Sexual Magnet

Your body wants to flirt. It's a very natural thing. If you are attracted to someone, your body will express that reaction—but only if you let it out of its cage. Bodies don't lie. I was at a party with my friend Elise and we were surrounded by over a hundred available lesbians. Elise was standing in a corner with her coat draped in front of her and her arms crossed. She said to me, "I really want to meet someone." Her *words* expressed one desire, but her *body* was saying, "Get away from me." After all, how many women past the age of three months get picked up when they are in the fetal position?

Recognizing her dilemma and looking for material for this book, I asked her to try the following exercise. It worked! Within ten minutes, five different women came up to her. It scared her so much she went home.

Caution: This is a surefire, tested exercise designed to turn you into a sexual magnet. Do not drink alcohol during this exercise—it messes with the energy. And do not do this exercise unless you are willing to meet people. This really works.

Let's say you're at a party, a party full of potential lovers, and you want to meet all of them. Go off into a corner. Take a deep breath, then let it out. Close your eyes and focus on the energy in your groin. Now focus on consciously moving that energy up into your chest, as you did in the Stretch "Creating Sexual Energy" in Step 2. Imagine it as a color, and imagine the color swirling around your body. You'll find that you actually get hot. Now open your eyes, face the room, and focus on sending that heat out into the room. You will find that within ten minutes people will start wandering over to you. Try it. You'll be amazed.

GETTING LUCKY

Have you ever gone out with the goal of meeting someone and it didn't happen? When you come home disappointed like that, doesn't it make you want to take a long hot bath with a toaster? Well maybe you aren't setting realistic goals for what you want to accomplish when you go out.

Don't set yourself up for failure by giving yourself goals that are unrealistic. I've heard male gay friends talk of going out determined to meet the perfect "true love of my life," but as the evening gets later and later, suddenly the allowable is expanded. Where once it was only "blond, Nordic types, please," it moves to "men with hair"; and where "over six feet tall" was once a must, suddenly it becomes "men with two legs"; and from "under twenty-five," the panic escalates to "alive and breathing."

If you are finding that your nights out on the prowl are ending up with you feeling that "life is not for everyone," you might want to give yourself some goals that you have some realistic control over. For example, say that tonight your goals are that *I'm going to . . .*

- **get out of the house**
- **ask three strangers to dance**
- **talk to someone new, keeping eye contact with them**

- **give one person my phone number**

- **ask one person for their phone number**

- **ask someone out for coffee**

Whether the other person responds favorably or not is out of your control, but don't let that stop you from taking action.

Add your own list of possible actions that you might take.

1. _____
2. _____
3. _____
4. _____
5. _____
6. _____
7. _____
8. _____
9. _____
10. _____

STRETCH: Taking Action

Check at least two actions that you *commit* to doing tonight. Now, put down the ice cream carton, get out of the house, and take some risks!

REACH OUT AND TOUCH SOMEONE

Okay, so now you've got the hots for someone who is perhaps even more shy than you. How do you get the ball rolling when nobody will make the first move?

The only way to get physical is to get physical. Sometimes it's hard to cross the threshold from talking to touching. Here are some tips gathered from my gay and lesbian friends on the Internet.

- **Drop something by their foot and "accidentally" brush their legs when you pick it up.**

- **Prolong eye contact.**

- Put your hand on their leg while looking right into their eyes.

- Tell them they have an eyelash on their cheek, and very gently and sweetly brush it away with your fingers. Do this regardless of whether they have an eyelash there or not.

- Touch their arm when making a point.

- Touch their hair. "I love your hair. Can I braid it?" Do not, however, try this with underarm or pubic hair.

- While watching a movie, whisper to them. It gives you an excuse to lean over and touch them gently while whispering in their ear.

You'll be able to tell if they are attracted to you by how they respond to your touch. If all signals are go, it will be easy to move into the hug-and-kiss phase without getting a slap.

Okay, you've flirted, cruised, approached, and kissed. You're on your way to the bedroom. STOP!

SEXUAL NEGOTIATIONS
....

Whether you are going to bed with a stranger or a friend, presex licking has been replaced with presex talking. You've got to do it; your life depends on it.

"Being HIV-positive, I like to freak people out. 'AIDS, I hope I never get that again!' I even have a bumper sticker that says, 'Lose weight now, ask me how.'"
—HIV-POSITIVE COMIC AND AUTHOR OF *THE POWER OF HIV POSITIVE THINKING* **STEVE MOORE**

SAFE SEX HINTS
• condoms
• dental dams, Saran Wrap
• bad wardrobe

It's hard to protect ourselves from another person's energy, but it's easy to protect ourselves from another person's viruses. This negotiation needs to be number one on your list of things to do. And remember, just because someone has registered negative in an AIDS test, that doesn't mean they are HIV-negative.

Unless they haven't had unsafe sex for six months, you can't be sure, or too safe. Horny people can be hardened liars. And since you can't be sure, use a condom or Saran Wrap and keep it safe until you are sure. Your life depends on it.

"People keep telling me I look good. Pretty soon I'll be drop dead gorgeous."
—STEVE MOORE

"That was the V.D. clinic . . . just checking. You haven't been in lately . . . they thought you'd moved."

Safe sex, of course, is not the only subject two people need to negotiate before sleeping together. All major expectations need to be addressed beforehand. Don't make assumptions—get information. Otherwise both of you are going to get a lot of exercise jumping to conclusions.

TEST: WHAT ARE YOUR BOTTOM-LINE EXPECTATIONS?

Check which statements are true for you.

When I have sex, I expect that my partner . . .

❑ will marry me

❑ won't sleep with anyone else

❑ will let me call them at work

❑ will spend weekends with me

❑ will love me

❑ will give me gifts

❑ will see me again

❑ will know where I live

❑ will give me their phone number

❑ will call me again

❑ will stay until morning

❑ will remember my name

Sometimes when we have sex we also have a list of self-imposed obligations.

Now that I'm having sex I have to . . .

• give them presents

• call them every day

- **see them again**

- **invite them to meet my friends**

- **be nice to them**

- **be monogamous**

If you give your lover these checklists, be prepared for the fact they might check items different from those you chose. Having sex means different things for everyone. Where people get hurt is when one person is thinking one-night stand and their partner is thinking engraved wedding invitations.

I'm not suggesting that you have to know exactly what you want. I sure don't—what I want fluctuates more than Madonna's sexual preferences. I can wake up in the morning thinking I want a bridge partner and by breakfast I want a sex partner. Then there was the time I agreed to have a let's-just-have-sex relationship and ended up buying her a ring. Go into relationships with an open mind because nobody can really know what will happen. What appears at first to be a one-night stand can end up happily ever after. Be open to being surprised.

JOURNAL WORKSHOP: Sexual Negotiations

Write down what your expectations are today and know that they can change to-morrow.

_____

_____

_____

_____

_____

_____

Write down now what your bottom-line boundaries are (for example, no HIV-positive lovers; no anal intercourse, please, I'm never a bottom; no S&M, and if you try it again, I'll whip you silly; you will never know my address; no barking like a dog; no Pee-Wee Herman impressions).

I will not . . .

_____

_____

_____

_____

_____

_____

The second most important part of negotiations is asking what *they* want and need, and then actually *listening* to what is said. They will tell you everything you need to know. When someone says to you, "I'm not looking for anything serious," it is a waste of time to consider that a challenge.

"What a great orgy I went to last night!" is a good indication the other person is not going to be sitting next to you at church on Sunday.

There are always consequences to our actions, and if you really listen you will have an idea of what those consequences are going to be. I mean, is one night of passion really worth having a stalker on your tail? I think not.

DOIN' IT

"I thought leather was sort of like church. I worship it on my knees."

—BRENT CAPPS

It's up to you to create satisfying sexual encounters, and a great part of it is telling your partner what you want. If your lover doesn't have a sign with a palm

Things to Say During Sex

on it hanging over his or her front door, then chances are you'll have to speak up. "Left, right, touch me there—no, *there*—slower, faster, harder, softer, get that monkey out of here!"

SEXUAL FANTASIES

Do you find you are able to share your sexual fantasies with your lover? I'm not going to go into my sexual fantasies here, but let's just say I could be the Danielle Steel of lesbians—at least in my mind. In reality, I have Jewish lesbian sex, which usually starts off with two hours of begging: "Please have sex with me!"

Most of us are so used to keeping our sexual fantasies a secret because for most of our lives we had to keep our sexuality a secret. If there is anyone to tell our fantasies to, it's our lovers, but first we have to admit them to ourselves. And don't worry if your fantasies seem extreme; there are thirty flavors other than vanilla.

JOURNAL WORKSHOP: Sexual Fantasies
Get cozy and spend a half hour or so writing out your sexual fantasies in your coming-out journal. Try to come up with five different scenarios of what you would like to do or have done to you.

SEX TOYS

"It's not that I don't like penises. I just don't like them on men."
—LESBIAN COMIC LEA DELARIA

"Someone once told me to buy a Hitachi vibrator. I thought they said Hibachi. Boy, it was hard shaking that thing. But that was some fine barbecue."
—JUDY CARTER

Sex Toys are Great! I have no idea what men use, but vibrators are great for women. Let's face it, you never have to cook them breakfast. But ladies, be careful about using them too much and going numb. If you overuse a vibrator, you'll never find a woman with a fast enough tongue. You'll have to start hanging out at the construction site: "Hey, you with the hydraulic drill, what are you doin' tonight?"

Sex toys can really enhance sexual passion, but sometimes they can be awkward, especially if you're not mechanically inclined. My friend Ellen bought these anal beads, which look like Ping-Pong balls on a string. Apparently, when your lover orgasms you are supposed to pull them out slowly, one ball at a time. Well, as she recalled, she got so nervous that when her lover started to come, "I yanked them out as if

Robert suddenly remembered he had forgotten
to remove his cock ring.

I was starting a lawn mower." Someone called the police after hearing her scream. Moral: if you use sex toys, read the instructions and practice first.

Anyone who wants sex can have it. It's love, commitment, loyalty, and a joint mortgage that are hard to come by. If your sexual encounters (or lack of) are leaving you longing, you might want to try something else—getting intimate. Read on . . .

Step 5: Get Intimate

"The only abnormality is the incapacity to love."
—ANAÏS NIN

So now that you're out to having gay sexual relationships, is your lover throwing you out—out of the house? out on the street? out of your mind? You might have some intimacy issues you need to resolve.

Before coming out, many of us thought our relationships weren't working because we were masquerading as heteros. How wearisome to come out and find you still have relationship problems!

"I love him . . . I need my freedom . . .
I love him . . . I'm afraid of commitment . . . I love
him . . . I'm not ready yet . . ."

INTIMACY TEST

Do you have intimacy issues? Check those which apply to you.

❏ **All of my lovers end up cheating on me.**

❏ **I don't enjoy spending time alone with my lover.**

❏ **I feel uncomfortable crying in front of my lover.**

❏ **I'm interested only in people who would never want me.**

❏ **I totally ignore people I am attracted to.**

❏ **I have a couple of secrets from my lover—like, my marriage.**

❏ **I lose sexual interest in my lovers after I know their name.**

❏ **My lover relationships don't last long enough to get pictures back from one-hour photo.**

❏ **The lovers I pursue end up serving me restraining orders. I say "pursue," they say "stalk."**

❏ **My lovers don't tell me they love me, but then again, none of them speak English.**

❏ **I see my lovers only one day a week, because visiting hours are limited.**

❏ **I fall in love only with straight people, or at least they turn straight after sleeping with me.**

❏ **The only thing I learned from high school geometry was how to get into a triangle.**

❏ **Intimacy? Shut up and hand me my Prozac.**

❏ **My lover's pet name for me is "you scum-sucking pig."**

❏ **Lovers? I can't even get anyone to commit to my MCI Friends and Family calling circle.**

❏ **When making love, my lovers call out their own name.**

❏ **It's Step 5 and I still don't consider myself gay, but this is an interesting book.**

When I first found a female lover, I thought that was the end of my relationship problems. What a blow to find out that with women, I still had the same intimacy problems I had experienced with men. Bummer. Now, instead of complaining about men, I was sitting around drinking beer, going, "Chicks! Can't live with them." What's next? Animals? Bi-species?

And . . . how many of us, when our lover is throwing the phone at us, actually think, "If I were straight, I wouldn't be having these problems"? But is that true? Get a grip! Exactly what heteros are your relationship role models? Your parents? O.J. and Nicole? My survey says: Less than 50 percent of hetero marriages last, and many of that 50 percent are sleeping with us on the side.

Heteros can't pull their relationships together, and they get tax breaks, big cakes, and toaster ovens. So let's face it, all relationships are hard. They all start out with wonderful intentions of caring and loving, but then, someplace along the way, "You're the only one for me" turns into "Who is this person, anyway?" Even Billy Joel, who wrote, "I love you just the way you are," divorced. Most relationships start off with "Don't go changin'" and end up with "Do you have to eat like that?"

THEY SAY IN MARRIAGE THAT 2 PEOPLE JOIN TOGETHER AND BECOME ONE ... THE QUESTION IS, WHICH ONE?

Artist: Ann Glover © Judy Carter

In this step, I want to tackle a subject that has been dealt with in countless self-help books: coming out and being responsive to having loving, committed relationships. This step is necessary in a book on coming out because we gay people have homophobia telling us that we can't couple, we can't marry, and that our unions are sinful. Because of this, so many of us come out to being gay, to having gay sex, but not to being in committed relationships. Although there are gays who view monogamy, commitment, and marriage as hollow, hetero rituals, there are also many of us who are simply frightened of the consequences of committing to our lovers. For some people still in denial, truly committing to a lover would mean that they *really are* gay, and that's just too terrifying. So, many of us go from relationship to relationship, wondering what's the matter.

If you take into account all the extra stress that homophobia places on our relationships, I say it's amazing that so many of us ever find love. Not only are our relationships *not* affirmed by society, but many of us even believe that our love coupling can cause us to lose our home, job, and even our life. Actually, it's amazing that we gays couple as well as we do. It's amazing that we even get out of bed.

SO, NOW THAT YOU'RE OUT, HOW COME YOUR RELATIONSHIPS DON'T LAST AS LONG AS A BIC PEN?

Which of these relationship problems sound familiar?

- You're in love. You feel so alive, so awake. This person is *the* one. And then, six months later, you realize that you are in bed with someone who has the emotional capabilities of Cheez Whiz. And then comes the inevitable crash, when suddenly every song Whitney Houston sings is about you. Oh, the hurt! Oh, the pain! But you recover. And proceed immediately to fall in love with number two, three, four, and five, each of whom is also "the one."

- Or maybe you're the type who never seems to meet anyone who's really right. True, at first everyone seems great, but somehow they all become too tall, too fat, too skinny, too dumb, too poor, too unavail-able—or too available—to be with you. Hello, waiter. Soup for one, please.

- Or are you never the right one for the other person—but after being with you, he or she marries the next lover? You're never Mr./Ms. Right but always Mr./Ms. Right Before.

- Or are you the drama queen who worships the ground your lovers walk all over you on? "My lover trashed my car, emptied my bank ac-count, and slept with my best friend, and if he/she does it again—that's it!"

- Or perhaps you are the type that falls in love so hard that it's tanta-mount to being on drugs. You can't eat, sleep, or think about anything except your next fix of being with your new lover. You try to get off and go cold turkey because your life is going into the toilet. But after a few lonely nights you find yourself reaching for the phone. You're hooked. You are not *in* a relationship, you are *on* a relationship.

- Or are you great in bed but can't share much of yourself besides your body? "Take me, I'm yours. But touch my Beemer and you're dead meat!"

Of course, just about everyone has problems with intimacy in some form or other, but, growing up as a gay person in homophobic America, at a very early age each of us had to deal with strong feelings of abandonment and rejection. Homophobia taught us to keep our feelings hidden, because if we revealed our true selves, we would be rejected, shamed, and shunned. It is no coincidence that many of us have encountered these same problems when we get into relationships. Have you had any of the following complaints about your lovers or heard them *from* your lovers?

- **"You're not open."**
- **"Why do you keep secrets from me?"**
- **"You seem distant."**
- **"Why are you rejecting me?"**
- **"Why are you cheating on me?"**

It's no big mystery why the child who had to control her or his feelings becomes controlling in a relationship. The judged child becomes judging, and the child that had to hide their emotions becomes the adult that now hides their affairs.

Coming out to loving, not just lovemaking, is an extremely daring step of trust and a move toward total self-integration. All the other coming-out steps in this book involve coming out to the world, but until you feel safe within yourself, safe to love another no matter what their gender, you will always be imprisoned by homophobia.

Homophobia teaches us that

- *Love is about loss.* **If we fall in love with someone of the same sex, we run the risk of losing our family, our jobs, ourselves. Maybe that's why many of us at the first sign of conflict choose to lose our lovers. Perhaps the only thing anyone needs to lose is homophobia.**

- *Love is about blame.* **Our love is to blame for the decline of family values. But love is not about blame, shame, and humiliation; it's about honor, respect, and dignity. Yet when society doesn't honor our relationships, how can we? It's no surprise that the first one we are most critical of is the one who is lying in bed next to us.**

- *Love between members of the same gender is all about sex.* **Yes, relationships are about sex, but also about caring, trusting, supporting, and forgiving our lovers when they are late to a play, even though they promised to be on time and now the whole evening is ruined! Actually, sometimes focusing our attention exclusively on sex can limit the depth of intimacy. Let's face it, it's a lot easier to have sex with someone than to love them when they make those awful sounds in their sleep after they eat pepperoni pizza.**

The effects of homophobia are subtle, and unless recognized and dealt with, they can erode our ability to build a life with another person. Letting ourselves be a casualty of hate in any way damages our ability to love. Earlier in this book we dealt with the effect homophobia has on self-esteem, but unless we recognize the effect homophobia has on our relationships, we become its carrier, spreading its hate even to those we love. The venom of homophobia seeps even into the gay community, turning us against one another. We often become one another's oppressor. Look at the "Men Seeking Men" personals ads and see how many of them ask for "straight looking and acting only." Yeah, there's a relationship off to a good start. "We're gay, but thank God we don't look it."

"In the personals, when you see 'Straight-acting male seeks same,' they might as well say, 'Gay man in denial seeks other gay man in denial for fun and laughs.'"
—GAY COMIC MICHAEL RASKY

Listen on the street and hear how many gays trash their brothers and sisters. "What a queen; he's so embarrassing." "She is so butch looking I couldn't bring her home to my parents."

And how many gays become predatory homos, whose disrespect for coupling enables them to sleep with their friends' lovers? After all, if society doesn't value our relationships, why should we?

Besides keeping us separate from one another, homophobia creates dysfunctional relationships in another way. It pushes us into inescapable, unhealthy, codependent coupling. I know a lesbian couple so frightened of being found out that they have eliminated all outside

friends from their lives. They cling together in isolation because they have become so suspicious and fearful of the world.

Getting intimate with another person can be the most wonderful, exciting, and frightening experience in life. Yet how many of us settle for less in a relationship because of our fears? It's unacceptable to settle for less intimacy in our life just because we are gay. We deserve to be loved 100 percent. Coming out to having sex is one thing, but coming out to really getting intimate is a right worth fighting for.

TEST: IS HOMOPHOBIA CONTROLLING (AND LIMITING) YOUR RELATIONSHIPS?

Check which you believe to be true on any level. If you hesitate or are the least bit unsure, check it.

I believe that . . .

❏ gay people don't have as successful relationships as heteros

❏ gay marriages aren't as lasting as hetero

❏ gays can't create *real* families, as can heteros

❏ gays don't make healthy parents

❏ gay couples get too clingy

❏ gays don't get as intimate as heteros

❏ gay relationships are based on sex

❏ most gays (not me) have problems with intimacy

❏ gays are more screwed up

❏ gays don't stay loyal

❏ gays are secretive in their relationships

❏ gays have unstable relationships

❏ gays' relationships are more violent than heteros'

JOURNAL WORKSHOP: Homophobia in Relationships

1. Write in your coming-out journal how the beliefs you checked have affected your last relationship.

2. Are there any gays who annoy you because they look or act "too gay"? It doesn't have to be someone you know; it can be merely someone you saw on the street ("Oh, my neighbor is such a queen!"). Write down why these gays and lesbians bug you. What's the turnoff? How has homophobia influenced the way you feel about them?

3. Go back to the list of limiting beliefs about homos. Next to any of them that you checked, cross out the words *gays are* and replace them with *I am*, because the truth is, if you

A Lesbian Party

Artist: Ann Glover © Judy Carter

believe that *gays* are screwed up, then you believe that *you* are screwed up too.

4. Replace all your negative stereotypes and beliefs about gay couples with positive affirmations, and write them down in your coming-out workbook. For example, replace "Gays don't stay loyal," with "I am loyal."

STRETCH: **Take a Homo to Lunch**

Arrange to spend personal time with someone whom you find to be too nellie, too butch, or just too much. Get to know them beyond your limiting beliefs.

I must say that I had an attitude about butch women. In Vancouver I met this woman who was a big butch gal—short hair, men's clothing, tough attitude, the whole bit. As I got to know her, I found that it was my narrow-minded beliefs that reduced her to a stereotype. What a surprise to find out that this butch woman's bedroom was painted pink and came with a lace bedspread and a doll collection. And what a surprise to end up—on top!

HOW TO PICK THE PERFECT LOVER

···

When I found my first lover, I was so excited that I didn't really pay attention to whom I was getting involved with. So she drank her breakfast, disguised her voice when the phone rang, and had a probation officer; it made no difference. What did I like about her? She wanted me; that was enough. After many love affairs with women who started out nice and ended up psychotics, I decided to pay better attention before getting involved.

Remember, *nice* is a four-letter word, so beware. Everyone has fifteen minutes of nice. After that, it could be psycho time.

Ever notice on TV that when they interview the neighbors of the postal worker who just went on a shooting rampage, they always say the same thing: "He seemed like such a nice guy." And when they went back to talk to the people who had met serial killer and cannibal Jeffrey Dahmer at the gay bar, they all said, "Gee, he seemed like such a nice guy."

So when starting out on a search for that perfect mate, just remember that that beautiful, seemingly confident woman could have an unending pit of low self-esteem and that the gorgeous, sexy hunk standing at the bar could have a whole basement full of terrible secrets.

I sometimes think that Big Bertha gave us enough blood to operate our brains or our genitalia, but not both, or certainly not both at the same time. So when we get turned on, the blood runs out of our brains, making us stupid. In this age of AIDS, spousal batterings, and fatal attractions, one can't afford stupid. 'Cause if you do, next thing you know, they're cooking your pet bunny for dinner.

"I have no sense of what a good relationship is. She'd say: 'You stupid bitch, don't you ever leave the coffee pot on again!' I'd think, 'Oh, you do love me, don't you.'"
—LESBIAN COMIC COLEY SOHN

"Honest. My heart was faithful . . . just certain other parts of me cheated."

PSYCHO TEST

Check which kinds of lovers you've been involved with.

❏ THE DUMPER—We all know this person. Even Princess Di knows this person. They say they love you, repeating it as if it were a mantra. Sex is hot and everything is great, and then all of a sudden, your calls don't get returned. When you finally do get to ask them what's the matter, they tell you that "everything's fine." But their voice could freeze ice. You feel yourself getting desperate, even crazy. You've been dumped, without a warning and without a clue as to why.

"My lover was a pathological liar. He would say things like, 'Tonight, dear, we're gonna meet the queen of England.' Then it'd turn out we'd meet some *queen* from England.
—HIV-POSITIVE COMIC MARTY YEAGAR

❏ THE CONTROLLER—They seem so *nice* when you meet them. They know how to do everything the *right* way. And soon you will learn, after getting involved with them, that you have always been doing things the *wrong* way. They are only telling you that you're a "worthless piece of shit" because they *love* you. You start feeling diminished, unsure of yourself, but you can't let go.

❑ THE DRAMA QUEEN—High-maintenance lovers. No matter what is going on with you they have something more traumatic going on with them. You break your arm skiing? So what? They just got fired from their job. So you end up nursing them one-handed. Very often these people are performers. It's not worth it. You're better off paying the cover charge to see them from afar and keeping them out of your life.

"I called a lesbian 976 sex line and my ex-lover answered. And it was just like old times—she came and I cried."
—LESBIAN COMIC KAREN RIPLEY

❑ THE ENERGY-SUCK CODEPENDENT—They're fun, they're cute, but at the end of the date you are exhausted and you're not sure why. They call you up to see what's going on because they never have anything going on. They can be very expensive and will end up owning your car, home, and dogs before you can blink your eyes. These lovers can't be left alone. If you do they will find something of yours to keep them occupied. Usually sex with your friends.

MY LOVER AND I HAD ONE THING IN COMMON... WE WERE BOTH MADLY IN LOVE WITH HER.

Artist: Ann Glover © Judy Carter

❑ THE CONFLICT AVOIDER— These are the romantics. They are wonderful at creating a fireside tryst or at lovemaking by a deserted stream next to a cherry orchard in full blossom. You are in heaven. This is definitely it. And then you have your first disagreement. The romance goes and so do you.

❑ THE TRIANGLER—This type is never happy in a one-on-one. They're either pining away over an ex or sneaking out to be with someone else. There always seems to be a second person lurking in the shadows, or even in your bed.

❑ THE VICTIM—Listen to their sob stories. It can really bring a tear to your eye, listening to how their ex so betrayed them. But sooner than later you'll end up being another "mean, self-absorbed lover who doesn't understand" them either.

❏ THE ALCOHOLIC—"What happened last night? I don't remember. What's your name?" These are people who think sleeping with your best friend is okay if it was in a blackout. If you're with an alcoholic, you've got a disease too. It's Al-Anon time. Either that, or you've got yourself a drinking buddy. Cheers!

❏ THE YOUNGER LOVER—"Is that your daughter?" Forget about their not knowing where they were when Kennedy was shot. They don't even know that Paul McCartney was in a band before Wings, and even then they'll probably think you're talking about a TV show. Sometimes it's a little uncomfortable having to pick them up at their parents' house, but that'll pass. Soon they'll be old enough to drive themselves. Watch out when they start asking you for an allowance.

I DONT KNOW WHY ALL MY LOVERS TURN OUT TO BE ALCOHOLICS

WELL, MAYBE ITS BECAUSE YOU MEET THEM IN BARS

Artist: Ann Glover © Judy Carter

❏ THE VACATIONSHIP—You meet in the Caribbean. You feel so connected. You think you are in a *relationship*, but no, you are in a *vacationship*. Don't trust that the way they behave on vacation is a reflection of their normal personality. Sure, in Tahiti they're saying, "I'm a fabulous, free, loving human being who will love you passionately and unconditionally all the days of my life!" But follow them home to Wichita, and soon they're saying, "Hey, who was the asshole who unalphabetized my spices!" Bon Voyage!

❏ THE SELF-ACTUALIZED LOVER—Oh, will they love you if only you would let go of your *issues* so that you could be as self-actualized as they are! They'll give you books to read, take you to seminars, and arrange for you to see their therapist. They demand that you find God, or else they will find someone more spiritually aware than you. Don't expect these lovers to take care of you when you get sick. If you have an earache, they'll ask you, "What don't you want to hear?" And if you're smart you'll answer, "You!"

❏ THE DADDY/MOMMY—They are rich, and they buy you many gifts. They own a home with furniture! And how they promise they will take care of

THE
HOMO
HANDBOOK

101

you. And it's wonderful, but when you're bad they punish you. *Time out* is nothing to what they have in mind for you. Ouch!

❏ THE PROGRAM JUNKY—When you meet someone and they introduce themselves to you with, "Hello, my name is Pat, and I'm an alcoholic, compulsive overeater, vomiter, codependent, mind-control victim, Twinkie addict, and sexaholic," that means you've just met an addict—a program addict. These are people who go every day to AA, CA, and OA, but never seem to be OK.

If you get involved with one of these people, forget about having fun with them. These program junkies never have time to go two-stepping because they are always in meetings—twelve-stepping. And if you aren't also willing to go to meetings and sit on Salvation Army couches admitting your defeats, they will tell you that you are in denial.

If one night you have some friends over to play poker, you're not being sociable—you have a gambling problem. If you add a beer to that—you're an alcoholic in denial. And if you give anyone advice on how to play, you are a codependent—in denial. And God forbid you end up owing anyone money—hello, Debtors Anonymous. Don't try to change them, because you are powerless over their meetings as they make your life unmanageable.

JOURNAL WORKSHOP: Relationships

Ponder these questions and write in your coming-out journal.

1. What psychos have you been with?
2. Do you notice that you have a pattern in your relationships?
3. At the end of each relationship do you swear that, next time, you're going to pick differently—yet end up in the same movie, just with a different cast? How does that happen?

Sound hopeless? Don't despair. You *can* have what you want. But . . .

WHAT THE HELL DO YOU WANT?

Do you know what you want? If we don't know what we want, we get other people's leftovers, and if you're like me you probably prefer main dishes. So, in the great restaurant of life we must look over the menu and order before wondering where the hell the food is. Deciding what we want and then committing ourselves to getting it are necessary steps if we intend to fulfill any of our goals. Once we are clear, the energies that surround us tend to support the direction we have chosen. I'm not sure why this is, but you have it on good authority (me) that it works. For example, you're gay, living in the Yukon Territory, and want to be lovers with a cross-dresser who does a mean Barbra Streisand impersonation. If you fully commit to your vision, well, then, steady yourself, 'cause there may be a big queen with a page boy headed your way on the next dogsled. It could happen!

COME OUT TO WHAT YOU TRULY WANT

What do you want? Check everything you want in a relationship. Do not cheat yourself. Really go for it.

I want . . .

❏ **unconditional love**

❏ **deep communication**

❏ **intimacy**

❏ **respect**

❏ **someone I can trust**

❏ **a lover who is my best friend**

❏ **someone I can feel safe with**

❏ **loyalty**

❏ **someone who gives me space
without being jealous**

❏ **someone who gives me gifts**

❏ **someone who is hot for my
body**

❏ **someone who really listens**

❏ **to feel cared for**

❏ **to live with my lover**

❏ **no secrets**

❏ _____

❏ _____

❏ _____

❏ _____

❏ _____

❏ _____

❏ _____

Now let's take a look at your last relationship. Check off the words that best describe that experience.

❏ **Unconditional love**

❏ **Deep communication**

❏ **Intimacy**

❏ **Respect**

❏ **Trusting**

❏ **He/she was my best friend.**

❏ **I felt safe.**

❏ **We were both loyal.**

❏ **We gave each other space without being jealous.**

❏ **We were always buying gifts for each other.**

❏ **Sex was great.**

❏ **I felt listened to.**

❏ **I felt cared for.**

❏ **We lived together in harmony.**

❏ **We never had secrets from each other.**

OR . . . do *these* words more accurately describe your last relationship?

❏ **We were living hell.**

❏ **I felt suffocated.**

❏ **He/she cheated on me.**

❏ **I felt insecure.**

❏ **I was treated like a piece of shit.**

❏ **We couldn't talk.**

❏ **I got blamed for everything wrong.**

❏ **He/she told me I was fat.**

❏ **We couldn't live together.**

❏ **We fought all the time.**

❏ **911 was on speed dial.**

Was there a discrepancy between what you wanted and what you ended up with? What's up with that?

I have gone into relationships feeling that I've found everything I would check on that first list, but somewhere intimacy, loyalty, and great sex got replaced with "Don't you touch me, you lying, cheating, therapy-needing, insensitive oaf!" Of course I always saw myself as the good partner and my lover as the fucked-up partner who was trying to sabotage all that was good and loving. Finally, after more relationships ended up in the same sinkhole, I came to have an inkling that perhaps my intimacy problems didn't stem from the fact that my lovers were alcoholics, liars, or cheaters, or spit when they spoke. After all, *I* was the one who picked them. *I* picked them, *I* adored them, and then *I* didn't accept them. *The problem wasn't them. It was me.* After all, if I really picked some-one whom I could accept and unconditionally love, then I would have to commit to being gay, wouldn't I? So what if the relationships never got close to happily-ever-after? After all, I couldn't get legally married anyway. How advantageous, then, to pick lovers who would let me down but never lead me down the aisle.

Homophobia creates victim consciousness. We can choose to buy into victim thinking, or we can affirm that we are powerful people capable of creating what-ever kind of relationships we want. Once I stopped seeing myself as the victim of my lovers, I began to look at my relationship problems differently. I finally re-alized that making my life script work was going to take rewriting, not recasting. Rather than blaming my lovers for being untrustworthy, I saw that I was the one who wasn't trusting. My lovers might have been remote, but perhaps that was in reaction to my being an energy suck. And when I found myself in a love trian-gle, guess who was the hypotenuse—me!

Coming out to accountability means that we no longer volunteer to be vic-tims—in our families, at work, and within our intimate relationships. Sure, it might appear your lover is a controlling bitch, but if you are into being a victim, you can actually create a controlling bitch out of Mother Teresa. So if you have ever blamed your lover for creating relationships, you might want to do this next exercise.

JOURNAL WORKSHOP: Looking at Your Stuff in Relationships
Answer these questions in your coming-out journal.

1. What pattern do you see in the type of person you've been with?

2. How did being with this type of person serve you? For example: "Be-ing with a controller gave me an excuse for not running my life my-self." "Being with an alcoholic made me feel superior, and they had so many problems, I didn't have to deal with mine."

3. What did your lover do to create problems?

4. What did *you* do to create the problems in your last relationship?

5. What were you hoping for? What happened?

6. What didn't happen?

7. What did you get out of being the victim?

8. How do you allow yourself to be the victim in other relationships?

9. Do you put down others for pursuing their dreams? How?

10. **In your last relationship, no matter how brief, what did you learn about yourself?**

11. **How was the dynamic between you and your lover similar to your relationship with your parents?**

One way out of dysfunctional relationships is to stop labeling yourself a victim. Try this next journal exercise. It might be an eye-opener.

1. **Think back in your relationships to a lover who really hurt you—someone who really betrayed you in some way and caused you pain, someone who was a real shit. In your coming-out journal, write out what happened, or if you have a coming-out buddy, take about three minutes to tell them the story.**

2. **Now, retell the story without blaming the one who hurt you. Retell the story taking accountability for what you did to cause the situation to happen. It can be a real eye-opener.**

3. **Write a twenty-five-item gratitude list about your worst relationship.**

4. **Make a list of what you forgive your ex for.**

5. **Make a list of what you forgive yourself for.**

6. **Burn the lists.**

7. **Affirm, "I forgive and let go. I am free. You are free."**

REBOUNDING FROM OUR PAST

....

We learn how to be in relationships from our first relationship, the one with our parents. Every child is born loving, caring, open, and free. Then shit happens. There is always some event that shapes our beliefs about love and relationships, that will color and affect our whole future.

When I was five years old, my older sister, who was severely handicapped, was a ward of the state and was sent to live in a state hospital. This event created a limiting belief for me: *if I was less than perfect, I would be abandoned.*

So I got into relationships in which I desperately tried to please the other person, which was the only way I knew to stifle my fear of being abandoned. It's no wonder I chose unfaithful lovers who would always leave me, thereby affirming my childhood experience over and over and over again. Although painful, the experience was familiar, and each of these disasters also proved to me that I was "right" about not trusting anyone. But my inability to trust trapped me in a self-constructed cage of isolation. Needing to *be sure* and *be right* kept me safe. But it kept me alone.

I hit bottom. I had to admit that my life wasn't working. But the good news was that this sad situation was something I created. And if I was powerful enough to create my misery, then I could create something different. I started looking forward to what I could create, not backward to what didn't happen. I visualized what I wanted, prayed for it, and started to take major risks. Amazing things began to happen and continued to happen as I confronted my fears and learned how to trust.

© Donelan

"I wish I could go back to high school and apologize to Bobby 'Blowjob' Bronski."

How many of us have limiting beliefs, beliefs that tell us we are too old, too fat, too poor, and too gay to have what our heart desires? Don't buy into it. Come out. Come out and find love. It is so natural for you to have what you want. If you are open to it, you can find a love that transcends your history and your narrow definitions of yourself. Once you have come out to yourself—only then can you join another in a satisfying union of deep trust, caring, and love.

HEALING THE INNER HOMO

The homophobia we detected in the voices of our parents sent us many negative messages, one of the most damaging being that because we are gay, we don't belong in loving, trusting, committed marriages. So, obviously, one part of the solution in healing our dilemma with relationships is to heal ourselves. We must learn to love ourselves the way we want to be loved and to treat others the way we want to be treated. Once we love ourselves we become powerful and desirable in the eyes of others. We no longer give our power away and succumb to the negative self-images others would impose upon us. We all grow up taught to believe the "Someday my prince/princess will come" philosophy, basically believing that someone is going to come into our lives and rescue us. Well, look in the mirror: that person is here. Become your own loving lover. It all starts and ends with you. And it was there all along; you just didn't know it.

"Look at me: Growing up I always thought that I wanted to marry an athletic, rich man. And now *I'm* jogging and making good money. I guess I've finally become the man I thought I wanted to marry!"
—JUDY CARTER

JOURNAL WORKSHOP: Limiting Beliefs About Your Past

1. What childhood events do you think may have shaped your reality regarding relationships?

2. What limiting beliefs did you learn from them and still carry about in your life today?

3. How are you creating your current relationships so as to affirm these limiting beliefs?

4. What are you getting out of the experience of relationships that don't work?

CONSCIOUS DATING

If you're tired of having relationships that don't work out, you might want to consider having a couple of dates before you hop into bed. The problem with sex with strangers is that you don't have the time to gather enough information about the person to determine the psycho factor. Listening to what they say during negotiations doesn't work, because psychos lie, and they usually are very good liars. It's people's actions that will tell you about them, not their words. And if you are drinking, you are going to be missing the clues that would tell you everything you need to know to keep this person out of your car,

© Donelan

"I'm dating a man of the cloth, too . . . of course, his cloth happens to be gold lamé."

your bank account, and, especially, your body.

One way to rewrite your script for a relationship is to date consciously. Growing up gay, most of us didn't have the opportunity to learn how to date. What were we supposed to do in high school? Put a note in Bobby's locker, "Let's go on a date after P.E."?

Artist: Ann Glover © Judy Carter

If you are or have ever been with a psycho, you had clues on your first date that you probably didn't pay attention to.

- **Big surprise that if your date was drunk on your first date, they turn out to be an alcoholic.**

- **Major wonder that the date who kept sending back his or her entrée was picky in bed.**

- **Big shocker that the person who excessively uses the words *I* and *me* in their first conversation with you can't remember your birthday or your last name.**

- **Big news that the person who orders for you in the restaurant ends up ordering you around.**

- **Hot flash that the person who spends the first date trashing their ex will, in a relationship, trash you.**

- **No shit that the person who comments on the large quantities of food you eat winds up being overly critical of your body.**

- **Good morning that the person who insists on driving ends up being controlling.**

- **Wake up and smell the coffee that the person who accidentally slashes your wrist with a steak knife is into bondage.**

- **Small wonder that the person who, on your first date, checking themselves out in the mirror on the dance floor had a mirror over their bed and, while making love, kept telling you that you were blocking their view.**

So if you pry your brains loose of your crotch and start dating consciously, you will pick a better lover.

We have an entire community who missed out on the relationship training known as teenage dating. Especially we lesbians. Even those of us who were hetero in high school learned that it was the guy who did everything, like deciding where we were going, what we were going to eat, and when he would pick us up. Initially, going on a date with a woman was frightening to me. Who calls whom? I wondered. Who pays? If I pay, why? If she pays, what does that mean?

Many of my friends have never even gone on dates. In the sixties, nobody dated. After an exhausting day of protesting the war, we smoked pot and fucked. Now we find ourselves in our forties and have just starting dating, while emotionally we are sixteen years old and still wondering who should open the car door.

How many of us use dating to impress, manipulate, and get someone into bed? Or how many of us skip dating and head right into bed . . . or an alley? How many of us drink on our dates and then, six months later, find ourselves in a relationship with someone we don't know and wonder why we made such a bad choice? Good morning! It doesn't have to be that way. There *is* an alternative. Dating doesn't have to be boring, scary, or exhausting. It can be an eye-popping stretch if we are willing to move our butts out of our comfort zone.

DATING TO LEARN ABOUT *THEM*

"Every move you make, every breath you take, every vow you break, I'll be watching you."
—STING

Dating Tips

Listen to the way they have treated others they have dated, or maybe even with whom they have had relationships, because it's exactly the way they'll treat you.

Listen to what they say they want, and compare that to their actual behavior.

- **Do they say they want openness but act like they're in the witness protection program?**

- **Do they say they want to trust, but you discover they have a copy of your TRW credit report?**

- **Do they say they want to be close but never take off their coat?**

Watch the way they dance because, most likely, it's exactly the way they will be in bed. If he's real good at the hustle, then he might be one!

Watch them around food. Do they order steak and potatoes in a Chinese restaurant? Do they ask for sushi well done? They may not be as sophisticated or as open to new experiences. How do they order? If making dinner choices puts them on overload, committing to a relationship might just push them over the edge. And watch how they eat. Do they eat slowly, indulging in the sensual pleasures of the meal, or do they just shovel it in, unaware of what they are eating? I like my lovers to be very aware of what they are eating, especially if it's me.

Ask them about their mother. Nobody has had a perfect childhood, but it's not what happened to them but how they have dealt with it. Did their mother have a drinking problem? Did they triumph over their past, or let it beat them down? Do they have the desire for sedation, or the quest for growth? Do they go to Al-Anon, or do they go to beer busts?

DATING TO LEARN ABOUT *YOU*

Okay, so chances are, when you're dating, you tell the story of one of your psycho lovers. And the story usually goes like this: "Boy, did he/she betray me, lie to me, con me, cheat on me, rob me, hurt me, and I'll pick better next time."

So you date like Nancy Drew, looking for clues that this person is going to be different. And they seem like they are, and *boom!* there you are again in the same situation. Perhaps you need to change *your* dating MO.

TEST: WHAT IS YOUR DATING MO?

On your last date did you

❑ drink?

❑ have sex right away?

❑ spend money on *her?*

❑ let her spend money on *you?*

❑ tell him about your venereal warts—on the first date—and you're a guy?

❑ wear—on your first date—your elastic waist-eating pants?

❑ pretend to be into things that you're not? ("I just find stamp collecting so sexy!")

❑ lie about your age? ("Sean Lennon's father was a musician? Really?")

❑ tell a sob story about your last relationship, blaming your ex? ("It was her fault I cheated.")

❏ make all the plans? ("No, I'm not controlling.")

❏ play hard to get? ("Movie Saturday? Well, if I'm there and you're there, maybe; we'll see.")

❏ turn into Vickie Carr waiting for them to call you, rather than you calling them? ("Let it please be them . . . Oh God, oh God. It must be them or I shall die!")

❏ pretend you just threw together the outfit? ("Oh, this old $800 designer thing?")

❏ act casual even though you are totally flipped out about dating?

❏ pretend you're not attracted to him/her when you are so hot?

❏ *Dating? I've never done it. I just move in.*

Look at what you checked above and write in your coming-out journal what childhood beliefs you are recreating through your dating behavior.

STRETCH: Making Different Choices

Remember, if you always do what you've always done, you'll always get what you've always gotten. If you want something different, you've got to try something different. The question is, are you really willing to risk it?

- **If you always drink on a date, would you consider dating sober?**

- **If you always talk about yourself, how about asking your date questions about her- or himself?**

- **If you are always the one to wait for someone to call you, how about you making the call?**

- **If you talk constantly, how about shutting up for a while and listening for a change?**

- **If you always have sex right away, how about keeping your pants on for a change?**

- **If you usually present yourself as perfect, how about relaxing a little— scratch when it itches, belch when you gotta? (Act yourself. Let's face it, eventually they're just going to find out you're defective like everyone else.)**

If you think of dating as the chore you have to endure before sex, you might want to try doing something different on a date, or at least vary the usual sip, sup, slobber routine. Because gay sex was so taboo for so long, just the mention that someone was gay made me think about sex. It was always my first thought. But as all my "in love" relationships turned out to be "in lust," I decided to try something different—waiting. I dated my lover for three months before we *did it*. Okay, the truth was, she was out of the country for one of those months, and I had a cold sore for the other two. But truthfully, it was frustrating, scary, and one of the most rewarding things I ever did. I got an opportunity to see how I was using sex to avoid intimacy. When we finally made love, it was my first time being with someone who was a friend first.

And if you think that dating without sex is boring, you might be arranging boring dates. Do you always go to restaurants? Sometimes those restaurant dates can be like going on a bad job interview—with bread sticks. Instead, try to do things on dates that reveal your passions, something that can be shared, like skiing, art walks, or taxidermy.

Write five different choices you could make on your next date:

1. _____
2. _____
3. _____
4. _____
5. _____

JOURNAL WORKSHOP: Recap Your Date

Go on a date, and afterwards, using the third-person approach, write out what happened. If your name is John, write, "John decided not to drink when he went out with Ron. When John picked Ron up, he was scared, but . . ."

Now answer these questions:

- **What is your usual MO on a date?**

- **What did you do this time that was different?**

- **What did your date say or do that revealed things about her or him?**

- **How did you feel about this person?**

- **What was your interaction like?**

- **What different choices can you make on your next date?**

GETTING COMMITTED
· ·

Committing to another person is an act of trust. And with homophobia telling us we are untrustworthy, how can we trust that gay person in bed with us? How can we trust ourselves? Buying that ring and putting it on your lover's finger is not only a leap of faith but an act of revolution. It's saying that we can have it all—the wedding cake, the children, the family, the house with the picket fence.

"Here's how you talk dirty to somebody you've been with for nine years. 'I'm going to take off all your clothes . . . and put them in the hamper.'"
—LESBIAN COMICS AND WRITERS SARA CYTRON AND HARRIET MALINOWITZ

JOURNAL WORKSHOP: Commitment Fears

1. **Write down what you fear about asking your lover to marry you. What does it mean if you make that kind of commitment?**

    - **That I'm really gay?**
    - **That I'll lose myself?**
    - **That they'll hurt me?**
    - **That I'll never be able to seduce a stranger as long as I live?**

2. **What hetero fantasies are you holding on to that prevent you from joining in a committed, loving relationship?**

"Okay . . . Okay . . . maybe I don't *love* you. . . .
Maybe I just *like* you . . . okay?"

    - **Girls at work giving you a shower?**
    - **Parents giving you away? (Except in this case they might not want you back.)**
    - **Official recognition?**
    - **Spousal benefits?**
    - **Not the same honeymoon treatment from hotels? (You might not find a bowl of fruit and some champagne.)**
    - **No listing of your engagement in the *Christian Science Monitor*?**
    - **Cuisinart at your bridal shower?**

- **Children? Being on *The Newlywed Game*?**
- **Making your parents happy?**

3. **Imagine you and your lover are getting married. Go into detail—the outfit, who's there, including each member of the accordion band. Write it all down. How does that make you feel? Does it scare you? If so, why?**

COMING OUT AS A COUPLE

"The Homosexual Couple—An openly professed homosexual couple should be considered a social entity and be invited to social functions on one invitation. Their names would be listed alphabetically on separate lines."
—AMY VANDERBILT

The final step in coming out to intimacy is taking pride in your relationship and coming out as a couple. Identifying yourself as a same-sex couple is a big commitment. It's easy to say I'm not really gay when I'm alone, but making a commitment to another person means making a commitment not only to that individual but to being gay

and letting go of all those hetero fantasies rooted in homophobia.

Growing up, it is impossible to escape the images of having a hetero family, since most of us grow up in one. But since Stonewall and the emergence of gay culture, we gays have redefined these images. We now have big weddings, raise children, and go to PTA meetings as copartners.

Not being out and fear of being outed might adversely affect your intimacy with your lover. Relationships are tough enough, but relationships based on lying can become isolated, distant, and codependent.

I had a lover, Amy, who was frightened of anyone knowing about us. It was torturous for me to put a brake on my natural, spontaneous inclinations to express love. I got paranoid having to look around, making sure the coast was clear before I touched her, kissed her, or even looked at her. No wonder it became hard to turn that spontaneity back on like a light switch when we were finally alone.

I also began to feel controlled by her, because all exchanges of affection were based on her rules, her fears. I began to feel less than secure as I took it all personally. I found that my writing and creativity were also being harmed as I started shutting down *all* spontaneous inclinations. I felt that she was ashamed of our relationship, ashamed of being gay, and ashamed of me. I felt unloved and—guess what, big surprise—the relationship fell apart. I was treated as if I were the clapper. "Clap on, clap off." Eventually I did clap off for good.

Now, looking back at the relationship, I see that I chose her because I wasn't ready to come out and be open. That relationship was a powerful step for me toward writing this book. It revealed to me just how oppressive it is being in the closet.

All relationships take courage, faith, and love, and you can't be in faith and in fear at the same time. If you are not out, you are in fear. And what is that fear? The fear of exposure? The fear of love? You can't honor homophobia and honor your lover at the same time. One will have to go by the wayside.

TEST: "LOVER? THAT'S MY ROOMMATE."

Are you out as a couple?

❑ Do your coworkers think you're single?

❑ Do you participate as a couple with your straight friends?

❑ Do you come to your office Christmas party alone?

❑ Do you have the extra, "This is his/her bedroom" room in your house?

❑ Is your lover's birthday acknowledged by your family?

❑ Do you still let people fix you up on hetero dates?

❑ Do you still refer to your lover as being of a different gender?

❑ Have you had a commitment ceremony?

❑ Do you show physical affection in the house only with the shades drawn, all doors locked, and your security system on?

JOURNAL WORKSHOP: **Coming Out As a Couple**

1. In your current (or last) relationship, in what ways aren't (weren't) you out as a couple?

2. How does (did) not being out affect your relationship and your level of commitment?

3. Imagine that you're getting married. Go into detail—the outfit, the music, the strippers. Write for five minutes. How does that make you feel? Does it scare you? If so, why?

STRETCH: **Coming Out As a Couple**

Pick one of the following to do as a Stretch.

- **Hold hands as you walk down the street with your lover.**
- **Use the words *life partner*.**
- **Get married in front of your family.**
- **Use the word *we* even when speaking to the hets.**
- **Have a romantic dinner out at a restaurant, holding hands.**

Coming out as a couple is a powerful step. And it can start with coming out to your friends. *Your straight friends.*

Step 6: Tell Your Straight Friends

So, you think you're out? "Yeah I'm out. Everyone I've slept with knows I'm queer." Oh, how daring of you. Did you also reveal to the people you work with that you're a secretary? Wow.

Why are we so frightened to tell our straight friends that we are gay? After all, with the exception of certain heteros like Rush Limbaugh, Newt Gingrich, and Anita Bryant, they're not a bad lot if you give them a chance.

"Why do you think homosexuals are called fruits? It's because they eat the forbidden fruit of the tree of life . . . which is male sperm . . . There is even a Jockey short called Forbidden Fruit. Very subtle. Did you know that?"
—ANITA BRYANT

The truth is, most of us are afraid that if we come out to our friends they will reject us. We learn from our earliest childhood experiences that if we want to be a part of the group, we have to conform. Let's face it, how many of us found kindergarten cliques that were just right for girls who wanted to play football, or for boys who wanted to play with dolls? We learn early on that to be honest— both to our friends and to ourselves—can lead to alienation, rejection, and a lot of pain. So, no wonder we have trouble coming out to friends—it is an act of supreme courage.

In coming out so publicly, I've lost some friends and gained others, but my closest straight friend, Leslie, is still my best friend. Although we have different sexual orientations, we have a lot in common. We both love the same movies, we

TEST: ARE YOU OUT TO YOUR STRAIGHT FRIENDS?

THE
HOMO
HANDBOOK
....
119

❏ **Have you come out to just a few, select friends and do you find you're having trouble remembering who knows and who doesn't?**
All of a sudden pronouns get mixed up. "Oh, I'm in love with her, I mean him . . . them." Great, so now your friends think you're involved with a *group* of lovers.

❏ **Are you having a hard time telling your *old* friends?**
Whether by choice or circumstance, you haven't seen an old friend for a long time. Actually, the last time you guys talked, you were straight. Or thought you were straight. So, when your friend asks you, "What's new?" you flip out inside. What do you say? "Oh, nothing much. I bought a new sweater, I've become a homo, my dog has fleas."

❏ **Do you have a hard time telling a *new* friend?**
You've met someone who has become a friend. You find that you have a lot in common, except your sexuality. When you first met, he/she asked if you were married, and although you've been living with your lover for four years, you said, "Well, no, I'm not married . . ."

You may actually have hesitated for a moment, weighing whether you should seize this moment to come out, but you didn't, and the window of opportunity closed as the subject changed. In the continuing time you've spent together, your new friend has revealed much about her- or himself to you—intimate things, such as the fact that he watches erotic videos, shaves his shoulders, and has two lovers, while the only intimate thing you've revealed about yourself is your passion for stamp collecting.

You hope your friend will ask you something that will give you an opening to set the record straight (so to speak). But it doesn't happen. As time passes, you begin to feel fraudulent, but you keep hoping that the friend will ask, and when he does, you'll tell.

❏ **Have you segregated your life?**
Christmas is spent with your straight family and Halloween is spent with your gay family. Saturday night, spent out dancing, is gay, and Monday morning, at work, is straight.

❏ **Since coming out, have you become heterophobic, eliminating straight friends from your close circle? Have you become a breeder basher?**

both cry a lot, and we both have a tendency to pick lovers with the emotional depth of Velveeta.

Actually, in my life, lovers have come and gone, but my friends have remained a solid support for me. We nurse one another through our breakups, fix one another up, and gather around one another at holidays. For so many of us who are away from our birth families, emotionally or physically, our friends are our family.

It's also stupid to let go of friends just because they are straight. After all, it's easier to find a lover than a friend.

- **A friend will never say, "Let's just be friends."**
- **A friend won't leave you just because she's found another friend.**
- **A same-sex straight friend won't sleep with your lover.**
- **A straight friend can be of great assistance at bars. Prospective pickups flock to straight people, who can turn them on to you.**

Straight friends—don't leave home without them!

WHAT ARE YOUR EXCUSES FOR NOT COMING OUT TO HETEROS?

❏ **"She/he doesn't really live nearby, so why bother with it?"**

❏ **"He/she won't get it."**

❏ **"I see them only a couple of times a year, and they don't have to know."**

❏ **"They'll reject me."**

❏ **"They won't let me be around their kids."**

❏ **"They'll tell my boss."**

❏ **"They'll blab all over town about me."**

❏ **"I can't tell *that* friend. He's a Shriner. He wears those funny hats!"**

Sometimes the person that seems the most impractical to tell will give you the most gain. Perhaps that person is in your life to give you this opportunity to confront your fears. Gay people are forever having to be brave. Face it, we are modern-day heroes, risking it all for truth, justice, and the American way. That's why I know that Superman was gay. He never slept with Lois Lane, and let's face it, who else but a fag would have the balls to wear that outfit?

1. Make a list of the friends in your life today, putting a star next to those who know you are gay.

2. Among those who don't know, who are the easy ones to come out to?

3. Who are the scary ones?

4. Pick the scariest friend to come out to, and write the ten worst things that could happen if you came out to her or him.

5. What do you have to gain by telling that person?

6. If you are being secretive around your friends, how is that secrecy affecting your relationships?

7. If you are in the closet around friends, how does that affect the way you feel about yourself?

You might not feel *ready* to take this coming-out step. That's okay. Timing is a magical thing. I don't know how to *be ready* to take actions. I do know that if you wait for your fears to subside, you'll be ready to go into a coffin before being ready to come out to the world. I knew I had to come out before I died, because the idea of being bundled by a straight undertaker in a pink chiffon dress for all eternity was more than I could handle.

TOP REASONS FOR *NOT* COMING OUT TO HETERO FRIENDS

On the basis of questionnaires, here are some of the most common fears about coming out to friends.

Excuse #1: "I'm frightened that my straight friends will reject me."
Through the years, some of my biggest disappointments have come from friends I really cared about who couldn't accept me, and who have fallen by the wayside in my growth process. The hard part about coming out and experiencing personal growth is having to let go of those friends. But the question you have to ask yourself is, If someone can't accept who you are, are they really a friend?

Perhaps your friendships have been based on a silent agreement of—"Let's pretend." Your coming out and taking on the challenge of living your life as an honest, open person might threaten these relationships, and in the end you might need to let go of them.

Sometimes friends are so threatened by your coming out that they become toxic friends. This condition expresses itself in a very subtle way. When you come out, toxic friends might say that they don't have any problem with your being gay, but then they get supercritical about other things, like your clothes. For example: "I don't care who you sleep with, but wear that fishnet tank top to dinner again, and I'm outta there."

After your coming out, some friends seem accepting but start verbally jabbing you, undermining your coming-out confidence: "It's okay to tell me, but you might want to be careful who else you come out to. Remember, you can't afford to lose your job."

You might notice that you don't feel *good* around this friend. You might suddenly feel somehow inadequate, as if you are too fat, or dumb, or just plain weird. Watch out! This friend has become toxic.

If you find that a friend is uncomfortable with your sexual orientation, perhaps it's time to move on. That friend has served a purpose in your life by giving you a reason for *not* coming out, or by supporting your negative views of yourself. But when you shift internally, when you move out of shame, all sorts of things can start to change—and *have to* start to change.

You might be able to work through your friend's irritating behavior by telling them how this negativity affects you. Hopefully they can confront their own homophobia and share feelings such as "Your coming out scares me" or "I'm frightened that if I'm seen as a friend of yours, others might think *I'm* gay." Many hetero people keep their sexuality contained. Your coming out can threaten them to such an extent that they feel the need to control you and herd you right back into the closet.

And if that happens, then you might have to make a choice between freedom and friendship. It's always sad to lose a friend, but that's sometimes one of the costs of growth and recovery. Alcoholics who go into recovery know this well. Recovering alcoholics usually change many of their friends when they stop drinking, and gay people usually change some friends when they stop denying. We get angry at these friends, at their inability to accept us as we are. We mourn them. We pray for them. And we (hopefully) forgive them. But whatever we do, we must move on.

Excuse #2: "I'm frightened that my friends will blab about me."

Another top excuse for not telling friends is that they will tell another friend, who will then tell a neighbor, who'll tell their cousin, who has a friend who will tell their bowling partner, who happens to be your boss's secretary, who will tell your boss, who will fire your ass, which will then appear on the six o'clock news: HOMOSEXUAL FIRED FROM JOB!

Coming out to straight friends, you might get the feeling that your coming out is getting out of your control. It is.

At a certain point, our personal coming-out process *does* get out of your control. The more people who know, the more likely you will become a hot item of juicy gossip. Hey, both homos and heteros alike love playing the "who's gay" game.

It is at this point that we need to have the willingness for our secret to become public. For, as long as we hold on to our sexual orientation as a secret, it will control us. We will be constantly worrying who knows and will become a slave to what others think.

To regain control is to let go of trying to control who knows you're gay and who doesn't. Some of us get caught up in trying to control who knows and who doesn't, and that leads to feelings of powerlessness and paranoia and to weird behavior.

Gay Paranoia

So, friends blab. Let them. Before, they probably thought you were a celibate dork. Take consolation in the fact that at least you have become interesting enough for gossip.

Excuse #3: "I can't come out to these friends, because they tell fag and dyke jokes. They're homophobic."

When coming out, you can be someone's wake-up call, launching them on a path of growth. When you don't come out to someone because you judge them ignorant, you aren't giving them a chance. A survey found that when people actually know someone who is gay, they are less likely to be homophobic. And if you find that your friend is truly a confirmed homophobe, then kiss them goodbye. Most of us are stuck with nincompoops as relatives—who needs nitwits as friends?

Excuse #4: "I don't want to come out to someone who is not really that good a friend."

Not coming out to casual friends, acquaintances, and neighbors will affect your life more than you think. Are you so nervous about your neighbors knowing you are gay that you and your lover or even another gay friend can't sit together on your porch in the morning? "Don't sit next to me, someone might see you." Oh boy, that really makes someone feel good about staying over.

Perhaps these people you are worried about are casual acquaintances and not close friends *because* you are not out to them. How can you have closeness with others when you are lying to them on a regular basis? Sometimes coming out can deepen friendships. Give it a try.

PREPARING TO COME OUT TO THE HETS

Have a homo support system in place. It helps to have a gay support team in your corner before coming out to your hetero friends. If the person you're coming out to is your sole emotional support, it might be too scary for you to let them have the reactions they need to have.

Use your homo support system. It is your safety net. What's so wonderful about our gay friends is that we all have similar issues. They'll most likely understand what you're going through because chances are they've been through it too.

- **Before coming out to a straight friend, let your gay friends know what you're doing and when.**
- **Rehearse your coming-out script with them.**
- **Have their phone numbers ready on speed dial.**
- **Make arrangements to see them the same day.**
- **Don't just crash by yourself after coming out.**
- **Have some Ben & Jerry's ready in the freezer.**

"Are you, like, sure her brother is gay? . . . He seems so . . . you know . . . normal."

© Donelan

STRETCH: Random Coming Outs

Before coming out to people you know, you might want to try coming out to strangers, people you will never see again, people whose reaction will not affect you emotionally. For example, come out to a florist: "Yes, these flowers are for Tom, my lover." Or a pharmacist: "My lover is sick, and these are for *her.*" Or to someone in the car next to you at a stoplight: "Do you know where the gay bookstore is?" Try it. It's liberating, plus it's fun.

I love mall outings. When I went shopping for a wedding ring for my former girlfriend, the saleslady said, "He'll *love* this."

I said, "*He?* I'm not marrying a *man;* I'm marrying a *woman!*"

Without skipping a beat, she said, "Well, of course you're not."

Which just goes to prove that most people don't care who we're sleeping with as long as the check doesn't bounce. So much for paranoia.

"Isn't it great? I think we're in love."

• **Give yourself a goal of coming out to three people today. Then write in your coming-out journal how you felt about your outings.**

"At the gym this big hunk asked if I could 'spot' him. I said, 'Sure! I spotted you the moment you walked in the door!'"
—GAY COMIC JAFFE COHEN

TIPS FOR COMING OUT TO YOUR FRIENDS

Tip #1: Initiate your coming out without waiting for friends to ask something like, "By the way, are you gay?"

The only people who *don't* go by "Don't ask, don't tell" are gay people who have the courage to come out. Most heteros are rigid followers of this oppressive decree. So if you are waiting for someone to ask you if you are gay, you might as well wait until Adrienne Barbeau has a comeback. It ain't gonna happen.

You need to take action. You've probably thought long and hard about coming out to a friend: planned it, rehearsed it, but waited. More often than not, however, we get outed by circumstance and then scramble to figure out how to get ourselves out of a jam. So your friend comes over unexpectedly and sees *The Advocate* on your coffee table or overhears your lover's sexy voice on your answering machine. When these things happen, "Lucy, you've got some 'splaining to do."

Don't settle for an awkward, on-the-spot explanation; create the coming-out moment.

Tip #2: Find some way to bring it up in conversation.

Coming-Out Icebreakers

- **Invent awards.** *"I'm so excited! My float won first place in the gay parade!"*

- **Use the word *gay* as much as possible when talking about your weekend.** *"Last weekend I went skiing with the* gay *ski club." "Sunday I'm going to the* gay *rodeo." "Tomorrow I'm walking my dog with the* gay *dog-walking club."* **If your friends don't catch on—then they are mentally retarded.**

- **There's the simple approach.** *"There's something I've been meaning to tell you about me."*

- **Or ask them if they have any gay friends.** *"Are you friends with any gay people?"* **If they say no, then say:** *"Well, you are now."*

- **Go for being funny. If you're a woman:** *"Remember when I told you about my new boyfriend? Well, her name is Dorothy!"*

- **Or there's always (if you're a man):** *"You know when I told you last week about how I had slept with at least two hundred women in the past year, and how I was beginning to wonder about ever finding the right mate? Well, I was lying. Not about the two hundred. About the women."*

- **If you have a political bent, try:** *"Did you hear about the antigay proposition in the paper? Being gay myself I find this campaign is very scary."*

- **Here's a good one:** *"Did you see the Oprah show about lesbian/gay go-go dancers? I could have gone on that show, except I can't dance."*

- **Leave gay magazines out on your living room table or have gay-related artwork on your walls. In my dining room I have a large oil painting** that has the word *lesbian* prominently displayed. I simply ask: *"What do you think of that painting?"* Hey, I figure anyone who makes their way into my dining room should know whom they are eating with.

JOURNAL WORKSHOP: Icebreakers
Write ten ways you can bring up the topic.

1. Leave the Homo Handbook on my kitchen table.
2. _____
3. _____
4. _____
5. _____
6. _____
7. _____
8. _____
9. _____
10. _____

Tip #3: Share with your friends how you feel about coming out.

"I was frightened to tell you." "I didn't know how to bring it up."

Tip #4: Reassure them as a friend.

This might be a time when you need reassurance, but a friend might need it too. After all, heteros are trained to find us scary. It can't hurt to remind your friends that they are important to you and that your sexual orientation doesn't have to change your relationship.

Tip #5: Tell them what you want.

"I want your support, acceptance, and love."

Tip #6: Accept them and let them go through their own process of dealing with their new understanding of you.

Whenever someone doesn't like me, is angry, or is in confusion, I want to "fix" them. I used to think that I was doing it to *help* them. Now I realize that whenever I have the desire to fix someone, it's because *I'm* the one who is uncomfortable. What usually happens next is that my friends get angry or frustrated with me, not because I'm gay but because I'm controlling.

We can support our friends through their process, but we can't do it for them. That kind of effort is not called help; it's called manipulation. Assist them in their process by giving them your ear, not your advice. Listen carefully. Respond when appropriate. Let them take the lead.

Everyone needs to go through her or his own process. You might be ready to tell your friends, but they might not be ready to hear it. If you sense that's the case, then let it be. I know, because I was one of those not-ready-to-hear-someone-was-gay friends.

When I was twenty-two and in total and utter denial about being gay, a friend came out to me. Even though I frequently went out with her and her girlfriend, and they kissed in front of me and held hands, I didn't have a clue. I was a putz. When she told me that Valerie was her lover, I became a cartoon character. My knees turned to rubber as I collapsed on the floor. I was aghast! I couldn't look at her. Because if I truly looked at her, I would have had to look at myself, and I wasn't ready for that.

Looking back, I understand that my friend's coming out brought to the surface all my own repressed feelings. It took a while for our friendship to recover. But it did. And when it did, it was deeper and more meaningful than ever before. My friend's courage to pursue her happiness led me to mine. Of course, she's now married with three children, and I'm a lesbian. Go figure.

Not all of our hetero friends will be able to accept what they perceive as a change in us. We may lose an important friend or two. But that can't stop us. We must be willing to risk our friends who have been significant because, perhaps for the first time in our life, we're treating ourselves with dignity.

Tip #7: Avoid getting hostile.

It's hard not to get hostile when coming out, because for so long we've expected the worst to happen. We've gone over the scenario in our head. "Okay, so I'll tell them and they'll reject me." As a result, they don't have a chance; you're already pissed at them for what they did in your imaginary coming-out script. So when you *do* finally come out to them, you may not do it in the most sensitive way. "I'm gay, and fuck you!"

Because in our minds we've already worked out a rejection scenario, we might start finding fault with our hetero friends and start rejecting them first. "I just feel we have nothing in common anymore because I'm gay."

You might lose friends in your coming-out process, but don't blow off a good friend because *you* are frightened to come out.

Tip #8: Deal with the sexual issues between you and your friend.

Sometimes straight friends assume that you are telling them you are gay because you are trying to get them to respond to you sexually. After all, all straights—and for some reason, especially the least attractive ones—assume that gays are dying to go to bed with them. Sometimes they actually get pissed off when they realize you aren't. "What's the matter? Don't you find me attractive?" (See the next section, "Smart Comebacks to Stupid Hetero Comments.")

But what if you *are* telling them because you are attracted to them? I've seen so many of my gay friends tormented by a crush on a straight friend. They scrutinize their friend's behavior, looking for the smallest of clues. "She invited me over for lunch! What do you think that means!" Most often it means that she's going to have you over for lunch, and the only thing that's going to be eaten is the Caesar salad.

My hardest coming-out situation occurred in telling a straight friend that I was attracted to her. Although she revealed that she was absolutely not interested in anything other than friendship, telling her helped me overcome my obsession for her. For two years I had hidden my desires for her, feeling secretive, detached, and even dirty. Coming out cleared away a lot of my guilt. I came to accept that nothing could be more natural than to be attracted to someone—gay or straight. On the other hand, I don't have to tell every straight person I find attractive. If I did that I wouldn't have any time left to do anything. But if it's a friend and I value the friendship, then it's something that has to be brought out in the open, or it will build a wall between you. Telling doesn't mean that you need to act on it. Besides, your friend is in all likelihood already aware of the attraction, and on some level is probably encouraging it. Sometimes talking about it clears the air and deepens the friendship. Sometimes you will lose a friend. And sometimes you end up happily ever after. It's a risk you might want to take.

Tip #9: Educate them.

Heteros have a lot of strange beliefs about us. Their ideas about gays come from a mixture of folklore, biblical quotes, AIDS, and porno films. Most of their beliefs about us are stupid. How many lesbians do you know who wear stiletto heels? And how many have long nails? And how many gay men do you know who don't drop their pants with just any stranger? (Well, okay, let's just say *some* of their beliefs aren't true.) Coming out to friends is our chance at educating this sorry lot.

"Lesbian porno isn't real. Real lesbians come home from a hard day at FedEx, they help you off with your work boots, stick in a tofu TV dinner, and prepare for lesbian foreplay. 'Honey, what do you want to watch tonight? *Thelma and Louise* or *American Gladiators?*'"
—GAY COMIC DENISE MCCANLES

Tip #10: Fuck 'em if they can't take a homo.

Not everyone is meant to be a friend for life.

SMART COMEBACKS TO STUPID HETERO COMMENTS

1. "It's okay that you're gay, but I'm not attracted to you."

If someone makes the egotistical assumption that, if you're gay, you must be attracted to them, you've got to mess with them a little. *Women,* say this: "Well, I'm not attracted to you either. I prefer women who are a little more feminine!" *Men,* say: "I'm more attracted to real masculine men."

It makes them crazy. Watch out. Women will start wearing a lot of lace around you, and men will start smoking Marlboros.

2. "Why do you have to make a big deal about it?"

"The Christian Coalition has spent millions of dollars trying to pass laws outlawing gay people from adopting children, kissing, eating in restaurants, having jobs, getting married, and holding hands. Exactly who is making the big deal?"

3. "What do you two women do in bed?"

"We play patty-cake and comb each other's hair."

I've noticed that they never ask gay men this question. If a woman asks me, I assume then that she's not getting oral sex. Duh! But I don't like telling straight friends in graphic detail what I do in bed. So I've developed a way to give someone the idea of what we do in bed. I tell them to find a persimmon. Slice it in half, then lick it slowly with your lips and tongue. That's one of the things we do in bed.

4. "I don't get it."

"Thank God, I'm getting it."

5. "Is this a phase?"

"Yes, it's a phase. I figure it'll last about thirty-five years. How long do you plan on being in your hetero phase?"

6. **"Are you the masculine or feminine one?"**

   "You tell me first."

7. **"You just haven't slept with the right person."**

   "I have slept with the opposite sex, and after sleeping with me, they turn gay!" "You're right! Do you know any cute homos who would be *right* for me?"

8. **"Why do you hate men/women?"**

   "Just remember—penis-severing Lorena Bobbit was hetero, and if that ain't hate, then what is?"

"They say that lesbians hate men. Why would a lesbian hate a man? They don't have to fuck them."
—ROSEANNE

9. **"Isn't it lonely being gay?"**

   "Why, no. There are at least seven others, and we get together each week to plan the gay agenda."

10. **"I'm pissed that you didn't tell me."**

    "I'm pissed that you never asked."

11. **"Why do you have to make things so complicated?"**

    "It's really not so complicated, because we have all read the gay manual and know exactly what to do."

12. **"I don't understand why you would choose a life of pain."**

    "It's not painful when you use a lubricant."

13. **"Why would you choose this kind of life?"**

    "Why did you choose to be hetero?"

"Now, dear, tell me . . . which one of you does, you know, the man's things?"

Lesbian Foreplay

"My best friend is overly protective. Every time I catch a cold, he starts crocheting me a quilt."
—HIV-POSITIVE COMIC STEVE MOORE

14. **"Have you been tested?"**

    "Yes! I got 800 in English and 530 in math." "Not all gay people have AIDS. I practice safe sex. Actually the high-risk group for AIDS is heterosexual women. The safest sex partner you can have is a lesbian or a nun—or, more likely, a lesbian nun."

15. **"I have a friend I want you to meet."**

    "Just because I'm gay doesn't mean I want to meet and sleep with all other gay people. But do you have a picture?"

16. **"Now people will think I'm gay if they see me with you."**

    "That will be an improvement, because now they think that you are a geek."

17. **"Why can't you keep it a secret?"**

    "Okay, I won't tell anyone you're straight either."

18. **"Why do you have to have those parades?"**

    "We have to get those batons out of the closet at least once a year."

19. **"That's really gross."**

    "Not the way my lover does it." "Gross? Sex with Tom Arnold—now that's really gross."

20. **"Can we still be friends?"**

    "Okay, but don't take me to El Torito's happy hour. Someone might see me, assume I'm straight, and ruin my rep."

21. **"I already knew."**

    "Why didn't you tell me? You could have saved me five years."

22. **"It's a sin against God."**

    "So is judging people."

23. *(To a woman)* **"You're a lesbian because you have had bad sexual experiences with men."**

    "If that were the case, ninety-nine percent of the population would turn gay."

24. *(To a man)* **"You need to see a priest."**

    "Know any cute ones?"

Now that you have enrolled the support of friends into your life, perhaps it's time to take a bigger risk . . . coming out to your parents.

HETEROSEXUAL QUESTIONNAIRE

THE
HOMO
HANDBOOK
....
133

If you are sick and tired of having to answer stupid questions, you just might want to give your hetero friends Dr. Martin Rochlin's Heterosexual Questionnaire.

1. **What do you think caused your heterosexuality?**

2. **When and how did you first decide you were heterosexual?**

3. **Is it possible your heterosexuality is just a phase you may grow out of?**

4. **Is it possible your heterosexuality stems from a neurotic fear of others of the same sex?**

5. **Isn't it possible that all you really need is a good gay lover?**

6. **Heterosexuals have histories of failures in gay relationships. Do you think you may have turned to heterosexuality out of fear of rejection?**

7. **If you've never slept with a person of the same sex, how do you know you wouldn't prefer that?**

8. **If heterosexuality is normal, why are a disproportionate number of mental patients heterosexual?**

9. **To whom have you disclosed your heterosexual tendencies? How did they react?**

10. **Your heterosexuality doesn't offend me as long as you don't try to force it on me. Why do you people feel compelled to seduce others into your sexual orientation?**

11. **If you choose to nurture children, would you want them to be heterosexual, knowing the problems they would face?**

12. **The great majority of child molesters are heterosexuals. Do you really consider it safe to expose your children to heterosexual teachers?**

13. **Why do you insist on being so obvious and making a public spectacle of your heterosexuality? Can't you just be what you are and keep it quiet?**

14. How can you ever hope to become a whole person if you limit yourself to a compulsive, exclusive heterosexual object choice and remain unwilling to explore and develop your normal, natural, healthy, God-given homosexual potential?

15. Heterosexuals are noted for assigning themselves and one another to narrowly restricted, stereotyped sex roles. Why do you cling to such unhealthy role-playing?

16. Why do heterosexuals place so much emphasis on sex?

17. With all the societal support marriage receives, the divorce rate is spiraling. Why are there so few stable relationships among heterosexuals?

18. How could the human race survive if everyone were heterosexual, considering the menace of overpopulation?

19. There seem to be very few happy heterosexuals. Techniques have been developed with which you might be able to change if you really want to. Have you considered aversion therapy?

20. Do heterosexuals hate and/or distrust others of their own sex? Is that what makes them heterosexual?

FAMILY OUTINGS AND OTHER GUILT TRIPS

By this point, I hope that your coming-out process hasn't been easy. If it has, then it means that so far you've come out only to your lover, your hairdresser, and a drag queen. Wow! What a risk taker! What's next, you little daredevil? A bungee jump off your front porch? The Mark Twain Riverboat Steamer ride at Disneyland? Ohhhh . . . scary!

If you thought that coming out to your friends was the big roller coaster ride, if coming out to your neighbor was a 6.5 on your coming-out Richter scale, wait until you come out to your family. The thrills! The chills! The nausea! Coming out to your family—in particular, to your parents—is definitely an E-ticket ride.

Mom sends me on so many guilt trips she should be a travel agent.

Coming out to parents is so exciting, in fact, that everyone should do it, even if they aren't gay. Let's face it, everyone has some part of themselves that they hide because they feel their parents will disapprove. What a glorious feeling to take off the mask of who our parents think we are and give them an opportunity to love us unconditionally as we really are.

In this chapter, no matter whether you end up choosing to come out to your parents or not, no matter even if your parents have passed away, considering the prospect of coming out to them might allow you to learn something new about yourself, about your childhood, and about the value of Prozac.

"It's a lot easier being black than being gay. At least when you're black, you don't have to tell your parents!"
—JUDY CARTER

"Did your roommate just say he was going to 'freshen his make-up'"?

TEST: HOW WOULD YOU FEEL IF YOU CAME OUT TO THE FOLKS TODAY?

Imagine coming out to your parents right now. Imagine that in your next phone call, you will out yourself to them. Even if they have passed away, how would it make you feel? Quickly check as many emotions as would apply.

If I came out to my parents today, I would feel . . .

❏ frightened

❏ anxious

❏ worried

❏ scared

❏ dreadful

❏ panicky

❏ disowned

❏ wrong

❏ abandoned

❏ rejected

❏ deserted

❏ alone

❏ angry

❏ hostile

❏ relieved

❏ peaceful

❏ hopeful

❏ happy

❏ comatose

❏ nauseous

❏ Hello? Dr. Kevorkian?

❏ free!

Chances are, if you haven't fully come out to your parents, your strongest feeling at even the mere thought of coming out is fear. Congratulations are in order. The good news is that if you have truly imagined coming out to your parents, then you've allowed yourself to feel some very uncomfortable feelings. Just by doing that you've conquered one of the major obstacles to coming out to your parents—not the fear of what *they* are feeling, but the fear of feeling *your* own anguish. Some of us will go to any lengths to avoid uncomfortable feelings, so we lie, hide, and move far away.

"Mom, Dad . . . sit down. We need to talk."

When we were kids, perhaps we were frightened of the bogeyman hiding in the closet. Now, as adults, we are still frightened of what's in the closet—only it's not the bogeyman, it's us. Even if we're long past the age of childhood, childhood fears come up when we just think about coming out to our parents. After all, there is a part of us that remembers a time when our parents were all-powerful, when our very life and health were in the hands of these two people. Scary, huh? In coming out to our parents, we get the opportunity to examine our fears and grow up. Okay, you may get cut out of the will, but you might also realize that you no longer need the allowance.

Although imagining coming out to our families can make us feel afraid, it still doesn't mean it's bad or wrong or stupid. Coming out to parents is about making a choice whether to let fear or love dictate

"Mother! Just when did you put bunk beds in my room?"

our actions. If you do the Journal Workshops and Stretches in this chapter and still decide not to come out to your parents, that's okay. Just the exercise of exploring why your parents make you feel like a powerless child might bring back the power you handed over to them a long time ago. Just consider: when you were a child, if they disapproved, they sent you to your room. No wonder you're so familiar with the closet.

TEST: ARE YOU STRAIGHT OVER THE HOLIDAYS?

Have you ever noticed, if you're not out to your parents, how hard those holidays can be? When going back home do you . . .

❑ feel the overwhelming desire to drink? ("There goes my ten-year sobriety chip!")

❑ pretend you are straight? ("Sure, fix me up with that blonde.")

❑ leave your lover behind? ("My roommate couldn't make it.")

When you're gay, *straightening up* when your parents come over takes on a whole new meaning. When your family comes to visit you, do you, as lesbian comic Kate Clinton says, *de-dyke* your place?

DE-DYKING THE LESBIAN'S CONDO

Gals, when your relatives come over do you . . .

❑ make sure *The Joy of Lesbian Sex* has its spine turned to the wall?

❑ put away those leather harnesses?

❑ replace that beautiful picture of a naked Melissa Etheridge with a Keane clown painting?

❑ turn the library into your lover's "let's pretend" bedroom? ("Oh no, the desk pulls out to a bed. It's a Murphy desk.")

DE-FAGGING THE GAY MAN'S CONDO

Guys, when the folks are over do you . . .

❑ take out the track lighting and replace it with fluorescent light?

❑ untie that Hawaiian shirt, button it up, and tuck it in?

❑ take the lube off the nightstand?

❑ replace the Jeff Stryker dildo with a nice lamp?

JOURNAL WORKSHOP: Giving Your Parents Power

THE
HOMO
HANDBOOK
....
139

1. How do you adapt to your fears of coming out to your parents?

2. How are you not yourself around your parents?

3. How do you avoid coming out to them?

TOP REASONS NOT TO TELL YOUR PARENTS

According to questionnaires, the top reasons gay people give for not coming out to their parents are:

- It'll give them a stroke.

- It'll give me a stroke.

- I'll be cut out of the will.

- They live far away and don't need to know.

- I'm not really close to them anyway.

- They'll want to send me to therapy.

- It will change my relationship for the worse.

- They're both currently on an iron lung.

- They'll cut off my allowance (although I'm forty-four years old).

- They'll want to go with me to gay bars.

- They belong to the NRA.

- They'll pull me out of Smith College.

Artist: Ann Glover; Writer: Craig Mills

"I wanted to tell my father I was gay but he was always cleaning his gun!"

JOURNAL WORKSHOP: Why You Don't Want to Tell Them

Write your top ten reasons for *not* coming out to your parents.

1. _____

2. _____

3. _____

4. _____

5. _____

6. _____

7. _____

8. _____

9. _____

10. _____

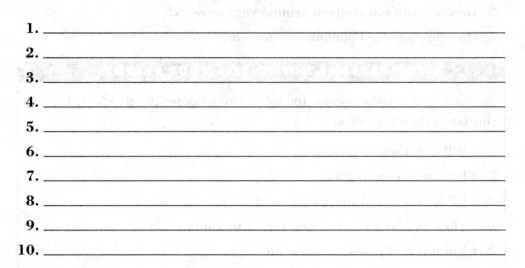

Artist: Ann Glover © Judy Carter

JOURNAL WORKSHOP: Fears About Telling Your Parents

What are your worst fears about coming out to your parents? Are your excuses realistic, or imagined? Do this next exercise by putting one of your excuses into *A.* Then let yourself imagine where it goes.

You can do this exercise in your coming-out journal, but it's best when done with a buddy. Face your coming-out buddy and look him or her in the eyes. Pick a coming-out excuse and run with it. For instance, if one of my excuses was "My parents would get angry," this exercise would go like this:

If I come out to my parents, *they will be angry.*

If they are angry, *they will have a heart attack.*

If they have a heart attack, *they will die.*

If they die, *I'll feel it's my fault.*

If I feel it's my fault, *I'll go on drugs.*

If I go on drugs, *I will overdose.*

If I overdose, *I will die.*

Therefore, *if I come out to my parents, I will die.*

Do this exercise with all of your excuses. Don't censure yourself, but really let yourself run with it. Say the first thing that comes to your mind, no matter how stupid it sounds. Make your answers spontaneous.

You might see, from doing this exercise, that so many feelings can start off with "They are going to be angry" and end up with "Someone's going to die."

Write in your coming-out journal.

"MOM, DAD, YOU KNOW WHY I NEVER MARRIED LOIS LANE. IT'S JIMMY OLSEN THAT I LOVE."

Artist: Ann Glover © Judy Carter

1. **Are your coming-out fears realistic or imagined?**
2. **What could be some realistic solutions to your fears?**

WHY DO WE CONTINUE TO LET OUR PARENTS RUN OUR LIVES?

Looking over your coming-out excuse list, how many excuses are about *them* and how many are about *you?*

"*They're* too old."

"*They* live too far away."

"*They're* Republican."

Do we make coming-out excuses about *them* because what we are really running from is *our own* worst feelings and fears?

"*I'm* too frightened to tell them."

"*I'm* feeling too guilty."

"*I'm* really straight."

It's interesting that so many of our excuses for not telling our parents are about how it's to *their* advantage *not* to know. We then play the scenario over in our heads: "If I come out to my conservative parents, they won't understand; they'll think I'm sick. They'll disown me. They can't handle it. They'll die of a heart attack."

And we then scramble to prevent the wreckage of our future: "So I'll just lie when I'm around them." Or, "I'll move far away."

We can get so frightened of the

possibility of rejection that we will actually give up the integrity of who we are because of this imagined scenario. Some of us pretend to be straight when around them, and, worse, some of us even go through with bogus weddings. (See "Supermodel" chapter. Just kidding.)

If you've completed the last exercise, you might have been amazed at how coming out to parents can feel as if it's going to be uncomfortable, and can escalate to where you feel as if someone's going to be hurt, get sick, and (in our worst fears) die. Or you can feel as if your coming out will cause their disapproval, and will escalate to where you feel that if you come out, they will kill you. Feelings tend to narrow down to *Coming out is either* (1) *"bad" for them,* or (2) *"bad" for you,* or (3) *just "bad."*

"It's not that my mom was overprotective or anything. It's just that when *she* had a headache, *I* had to take aspirin; when *she* was feeling cold, *I* had to put on a jacket. Thank God I got out of there before menopause."
—COMIC AND SCREENWRITER COREY MANDELL

Yet can anyone really predict what's bad for another person? And if you live in fear, can you really be a good judge of what's bad for you? Perhaps the truth is that no one can really predict or control how another person will react. In reality, most coming-out stories are filled with positive surprises and very few regrets or heart attacks. Mostly, the people interviewed for this book who came out to their parents said that regardless of how their parents reacted, coming out . . .

- **freed them from the burden of carrying so many secrets**

- **relieved them by getting everything out in the open**

- **freed them from the burden of lying**

- **created pride and confidence in who they are**

- **created more closeness in all their relationships, not just with their parents**

- **created unconditional love and understanding in all aspects of their lives**

If there are so many advantages to coming out, why then do we fear that coming out to our families will hurt them, when the only person we are really hurting by lying is us?

It's those damn dysfunctional families that we all seem to be from. In dysfunctional families, there is only one reality—theirs. And *theirs* is always right and yours is always wrong. Especially when parents are alcoholics, totally narcissistic, or just really screwed up, speaking the truth about yourself can have severe repercussions, creating genuine conflicts. For instance:

The parent says: "Put your sweater on. It's cold."

The child says: "No, I'm warm."

The dysfunctional parent says: "No, you're wrong. It's cold, and you put this sweater on before I give it to you good."

The child dares to repeat the truth: "No, I'm warm."

Then the really fucked-up parent says: "You do as I say. How dare you talk back? How dare you think that you know more than me?" And next thing you know, you're not putting on the sweater, you're eating it.

"When my mother found out I was gay she sent me to Juvenile Hall. That's smart. Sending me to live with five hundred girls who can't get out!"
—LESBIAN COMIC KAT HOWARD

This kind of dysfunction can really screw us little homos up. When children are punished for being different, they feel lonely and abandoned; it can actually seem as if they are going to die. There are only so many times a child can be trounced on for being "wrong" or "different" before they lose confidence in standing up for themselves. So, then, it's no big surprise that because, as children, we found simple self-expressions were dangerous, as adults we think that coming out can cause our demise. It's no wonder that when we know in our hearts we're gay, we hide—especially when the whole world is seemingly standing in alliance with our parents, guarding the planet against any expression of difference. Although it's lonely and dark in there, the closet is a very familiar place.

So if, in our childhood, honesty equaled punishment, abandonment, and even death, it's understandable that when we grow up, we transfer this equation. Our honesty equals death—not our death, but our parents' death. "I can't tell them . . . it will kill them." But what is coming out really going to kill?

Perhaps coming out is going to kill . . .

- **your fake persona**

- **your carefully crafted picture of what you imagined your family to be**

- **your image of yourself as straight**

- **your fitting into your family**

- **your being the same as your siblings and parents**

- **your denial of everything "being fine" in your childhood**

Face it, the person who wasn't real in all this is going to die when you come out.

JOURNAL WORKSHOP: Going to Your Funeral
Make a list in your coming-out journal of what you are letting go of by coming out. Now write down the ways your parents made (make) you "wrong."

1. *e.g. They call me selfish when I do things for myself.*
2. _____
3. _____
4. _____
5. _____
6. _____
7. _____
8. _____
9. _____
10. _____

"I had a nightmare that I was in a hetero family. Next thing I knew, I was dating Marvin Hamlisch and I bought a handbag. Thank God, when I woke up my girlfriend was next to me."
—LESBIAN COMIC COLEY SOHN

So, some of us grow up and move out of Kansas, but does that really solve the problem? If you grew up with parents who made you feel wrong, chances are you are playing the right-wrong game yourself.

- **How many of us would prefer "You're right" to "I love you"?**

- **How many of us make our parents "wrong" and hate them?**

- **How many of us make the world "wrong" for rejecting us?**

- **How many of us who have become parents are communicating this harmful legacy to our children, making our own children "wrong"?**

- **How many of us look at other gay people the way our parents do? "He's so Nellie. She's too butch."**

- **How many of us make our lovers "wrong" by asking them to act straight?**

Isn't it interesting that those of us who grew up with hetero gestapo parents who made us feel "wrong" treat others in the same, oppressive way our parents treated us? Some of us even have the balls (or ovums) to make our lovers lie. How many of us have become whom we hate—our parents?

I had the unfortunate experience of having to go to my lover's family dinner as her "friend." Before we arrived she gave me specific instructions: "Don't act gay." What exactly does that mean? As if I am going to eat dinner and then hump the hostess.

If you bring your lover to your family's home for the holidays, do you make him or her act straight? Do you give your BOYFRIEND instructions on how to *butch up?*

❏ "Don't offer to do my mother's hair."

❏ "Sit with your knees far apart."

❏ "When you talk with my brother, try to use words such as *pussy* and *dude* as often as possible. As in: 'I was out with the *dudes* looking for *pussy* the other day.'"

❏ "Watch football with my dad and avoid comments about the players' 'cute asses.'"

❏ "Don't call anything 'fabulous,' especially the drapes."

❏ "Don't do your Barbra Streisand imitation when we sing Christmas carols."

❏ "Avoid all words with S's."

When visiting your family, do you tell your GIRLFRIEND to *butch down?*

❏ "Don't volunteer to fix my father's car."

❏ "Don't volunteer to open tight jars."

❏ "Sit with your legs crossed at the ankles."

❏ "Avoid all discussion of Martina Navratilova."

❏ "Don't refer to your hairstyle as a duck's ass."

❏ "Don't lead when you dance with my father."

❏ "Don't bring up your bowling score."

Love, understanding, and acceptance—give them to yourself and you just might get them back. Write down some of the ways, big and small, you make others "wrong"—for example: "You don't squeeze the toothpaste *right.*" "You don't make love *right.*" "You don't dress *right.*"

1. _____

2. _____

3. _____

4. _____

5. _____

6. _____

7. _____

8. _____

So if you are avoiding telling your parents, you might think that the biggest obstacle is their narrow mind-set, but I beg to differ. Their view of the world may be restricted, but the true narrowness exists between your two ears. And if your excuse is that they live so far away it's not worth going through it, since they'll never find out, you might consider that there is some unfinished business back home that needs dealing with. Perhaps the real reason you had to move out of Kansas was not only to find other gay people but to be free to be who you are. Face it, we need to be able to be who we are everywhere, not just in Province-town.

Whether you perceive your relationship with your family as close or distant, whether you live with them or far away from them, it makes no difference when it comes to a childhood full of secrets. Moving away doesn't heal that child. Coming out can.

COMING OUT TO WINNING

In playing the right-wrong game, everyone loses. What would the world look like if nobody had to be a loser? "Who won the Super Bowl? Why, they both did!"

Imagine . . .

- **What if you didn't have to fight to be "right"?**

- **What if you let others have their misconceptions about you?**

- **What if you had empathy with your parents and realized that perhaps, if you walked in their shoes, you might be ignorant about gay people too?**

• What if it were okay for others to disagree with you?

• What if it were okay for your parents to be different from you?

• What if you loved your parents even if they don't give you what you want?

• What if you forgave them for being ignorant about your sexual orientation?

• What if you allowed them to find their own growth path, just the way you did?

• What if you affirmed positive things for them?

"Please, Amy . . . tell me there are two boys out in the car."

• What if you affirmed positive things for yourself?

• What if you so completely approved of yourself you didn't need anyone's approval?

STRETCH: Affirmations for Coming Out to Your Parents

1. Before coming out to your parents, you will need to get in touch with that little child inside of you. Find a private place. Turn on music that moves you. Sit still, close your eyes, and breathe slowly and deeply. Allow any emotions you might feel. If you find yourself crying, you don't have to understand why you're crying, and don't resist it. If you feel like moving, move. If you feel angry, hit something. Let yourself yell, scream, and talk. Get it all out until you are exhausted.

2. Sitting still with your eyes closed, imagine yourself as a child. Imagine one of those times when you were made to feel wrong. Imagine what that child is wearing. Imagine what that child is feeling. Ask the child what she/he wants. If that child wants to be held, wrap your arms around yourself and hold that child. That child is you. Make a promise to that child and affirm the following:

• I will always love you.

• I will take care of you.

- I will not let anything bad happen to you.

- You can trust me.

- You are safe.

- You are loved.

- I am finally here for you.

- I will never go away again.

Guess what . . . It's a done deal. Now—consider coming out.

"My dad calls me a fairy. I say to him, 'Hey, if I were really a fairy, don't you think I would have the power to date Brad Pitt?'"
—COMIC STEVE SHERLING

REASONS *NOT* TO COME OUT TO YOUR PARENTS

In my business of stand-up comedy, timing is everything. The same is true in coming out to others. Only *you* can truly know if you are ready to come out to your parents. Sometimes there are things we have to deal with before we are ready to come out.

- **Are you waiting until you're sure about being gay? "Uh, Mom, Dad, I think I might be, I'm kind of, sort of gay, but I'm not sure. What do you think?"**
  If you are still not sure, wait. Your own confusion might create even more confusion when telling them. Then again, sometimes the act of coming out eradicates our own doubts.
- **Are you going through a depression, anger, unsure times? "I'm gay and I want to die."**
  You might want to wait to tell them until you are on more solid ground, or at least until your antidepressants kick in.
- **Are *they* going through an especially hard time? "Dad, I know that you just lost your house in the earthquake, you lost your job, and Mom is on a heart-lung machine, but I want to tell you, I'm gay. Good luck."**
- **Are you financially dependent on your parents? "Mom, Dad, I want you to know that I'm gay, and I'm a grown person able to take care of my-self. Now, can I have my allowance?"**

• Are you waiting until you have a steady lover to come out? Do you think they'll think that being gay might be an aberration, but being single is even worse? "Well, I might be gay, but at least I'm not single."

• Are you not coming out because you don't identify as gay, even though you are in a same-sex relationship? You might still think it's a phase; or consider your sexual activity an experiment rather than an identity; or still try to date the opposite sex; or (my favorite) see yourself as an innocent straight person who was seduced into a same-sex relationship. "This is my gay lover. I'm not gay. I just happened to fall in love."

Such a person gets around any self-identity in coming out this way and presents themselves as a victim of love. "I *fell* in love." Yeah, what an accident that you just *fell* into that gay bar, and *fell* into dancing with a big homo, and just *fell* into bed. You're not gay, just accident prone. Right!

• Are you waiting for your parents to die? "Now that you're dead, I want to tell you something."

• Are you waiting for the *National Enquirer* to out you? "Mom, Dad, it's true what they write about me."

• Are you waiting for National Coming-Out Day?
Well, guess what. There is one! Use it.

COMING-OUT TIPS

1. Gather your friends around you before and after you come out. Plan this, so that you don't end up alone after coming out to your parents.

2. Have literature available specifically written for parents. Look in the Appendix of this book for suggested readings.

3. Call PFLAG (Parents and Friends of Lesbians and Gays) and see if there is a local chapter in your area.

4. Don't leave your parents stranded. Assist them in setting up their system of support. If you have an open-minded relative or friend of the family, you might want to come out to that person first. Then, when you come out to your parents, you can tell them, "Aunt Doris knows, and you might want to talk to her." (And perhaps Aunt Doris wants to tell them something about *herself*, too!)

5. Pick a fairly private setting, where you and your family can react and respond openly and honestly. It's preferable to tell them at their home

because if things get too intense for you, you can leave. If you tell them in a restaurant, pick one with soft booths. Coming out on hard chairs in the middle of the restaurant is dangerous if someone faints.

6. Be careful not to get drunk, like I did. I got so drunk that I couldn't tell my mother. She had to tell me.

"Mom . . . uh, uh, uh."

"Judy, is it you want to tell me you're gay?"

Then it was me throwing up in the bathroom, not her.

7. Give them time. It doesn't happen in one day. You are launching your parents on their process, and it just might take them as long as it took you to come to accept it. Hey, if it took you twenty years, give them at least a week!

8. Make a list of everything they might be thinking, and answer questions even if they don't bring any up. Bring up AIDS. Even though they don't mention it, most straight people think "AIDS" when they hear "gay," even if you're a lesbian. And if you do have AIDS, I would suggest you read one of the many books on the subject listed in the Appendix of this book.

"I came out to my parents at Thanksgiving. I said, 'Mom, please pass the gravy to a homosexual.' She passed it to my father. A terrible scene followed."
—GAY COMIC BOB SMITH

JOURNAL WORKSHOP: **Preparation**
Make a list of all the questions you imagine arising in your parents' minds.

HOW TO TELL THE FOLKS

So many of us get stuck in "How do we bring it up?" If your intent is clear, the words will come. What really counts is how you feel about it yourself. No one will remember the words. What will be remembered is the tone.

- **Are you coming from hostility, or love?**
- **Are you willing to allow them to have their own reactions without defending yourself?**
- **Do you need to be "right," or do you need to accept them?**

Change pronouns to suit your orientation.

- Blurt it out. "Mom, I have to tell you something. I'm dating a lesbian!"

- Put it into a list of bad things, and hope they won't dwell on it. "Mom, Dad, I ran over your cat, I'm gay, I'm wanted by the FBI for being a pyromaniac."

- "Mom, I'm singing in the gay men's chorus. That's right. Now you know about me. I'm a tenor!"

- "Mom, I have some good news and some bad news. The bad news is that I'm gay. The good news is that my lover is a doctor!"

"My mom doesn't understand that my boyfriend is gay. My boyfriend was sick and I told her that he was seeing a doctor. She says, 'Why can't you find a good catch like he did?'"
—COMIC CHARLES ANTEBY

THE COMING-OUT-TO-PARENTS LETTER

Some of the gay people interviewed for the book preferred to come out in a letter to their parents. The advantages to this method are:

- You can get it just perfect before you send it.
- It'll give them time to adjust before you see them.
- You're far away when they read it, and they can't hit you.

Whether you write a letter to your parents or tell them in person is your choice. If you do write them a letter, I would suggest waiting a few days before you mail it, and rereading it to another person to make sure it's from the heart and not hostile, and that it's as honest as it really should be. But sooner or later you are probably going to have to come face-to-face with them.

ACCEPTING YOUR PARENTS' PROCESS

Once you tell your parents, they are going to have to go through their own coming-to-terms process. It's like a death, in a way—the death of their idea of who you are and of what they expected: the big wedding, the in-laws, the grandchildren. Elisabeth Kübler-Ross describes the stages related to loss as shock, denial, anger, guilt, bargaining, depression, and acceptance. Some of these stages may last a long time, but some parents zip through them as if they were Evelyn Wood. Be patient, because when they hear those words *I'm gay*, they might at first go into shock and end up wanting to put you into electroshock therapy.

Stage 1: Shock
"My mother in Kentucky took me being gay really well. She can have visitors now. Not every day, but just a few at a time, the room is so small."
—GAY COMIC BARRY STEIGER

If your parents really didn't know, an odd kind of numbness can come over them: "So you're gay. That's nice, dear. Please pass the ketchup." Or they go ahead on automatic pilot, saying what they think they should say: "It makes no difference. We love you and we're going to bed now, even though it's 4 P.M." Or there is a big temper burst, and then they wake up the next day and it's as if you never said anything.

Just because they seem to say the right thing or don't talk about it at all doesn't mean that the process is over. It's just beginning. Let it be, and give them time before you talk about it more. They're in shock. But make certain that you do talk about it some more. Coming out to parents is not a one-day thing. It's going to be a lifelong process, and don't mistake acceptance at this point as a done deal. There's more coming your way.

"It was hard telling my parents I was HIV-positive. They thought the *HIV* stands for Homosexuals in Virginia."
—HIV-POSITIVE COMIC STEVE MOORE

Stage 2: Denial
At this point in their process, parents generally tend to go into gay amnesia.

- **"It's just a phase."**
- **"No, you're not really gay."**
- **"Son, have I got a girl for you!"**

Sometimes if you give them too much information before they can handle it, that will build up more defenses. But sometimes you really need to keep bringing up the gay issue around the clock to chip away at their denial.

"Mom, Dad . . ."

- **"I'm singing in the gay men's choir. Do you want to come?"**

- **"Look at that hot guy/gal!"**

- **"Look at what I got you for Gay Pride Day!"**

- **"It's just a gay day."**

Or if they keep asking you, "When are you going to get married?" you can answer, "Only a lesbian or an idiot doesn't get married . . . and I'm no idiot."

Or bring up famous people that they love or admire, and out them repeatedly: "Did you know that Malcolm Forbes, the millionaire, was gay?"

Remember, it all doesn't have to be resolved in one day. But do keep plugging away. It just might piss them off then, and they'll move on to the next stage.

Stage 3: Anger

Now they see that you might really be gay, and it pisses them off.

- **"You're going to get AIDS."**

- **"You are a sinner."**

- **"It's not normal."**

- **"Why do you have to do everything wrong?"**

- **"I'm cutting you out of the will."**

"When I came out, my mom said: 'Vickie, we would have never guessed you were a lesbian . . . you're so pretty and talented!'"
—TEXAS COMIC VICKIE SHAW

If you can stop yourself from reacting to their bait, they might quickly move out of anger and into the stage we all love so well.

Stage 4: Guilt

"My mom blames California for me being a lesbian. 'Everything was fine until you moved out there.' 'That's right, Mom, we have mandatory lesbianism in West Hollywood. The Gay Patrol busted me, and I was given seven business days to add a significant amount of flannel to my wardrobe."
—LESBIAN COMIC COLEY SOHN

At this stage you hear things like

To you

- "How could you do this to me?"

To each other

- "You shouldn't have given her the power-tool set."
- "You let him play with Barbie."
- "You babied him and turned him into a wimp."
- "You should have played sports with him more."
- "You taught her golf, and now look what you did."
- "Why didn't I *make* her wear dresses?"
- I told you you shouldn't have let our son dress like Zsa Zsa on Halloween."

Depending on what your parents' relationship is like, this guilt stage can get pretty intense as they blame each other. While they are guilt-tripping, it might be a good time for you to take that trip—out of the country. You can't fix your parents' relationship. Some parents get stuck in this state, but because it feels so uncomfortable, most parents get out of it quickly and swing back to denial or depression, or go on to the next phase.

I'VE JUST COME OUT

IT'S ALL OUR FAULT!

WHY SHOULD *YOU* GET ALL THE CREDIT?

Artist: Ann Glover © Judy Carter

Stage 5: Bargaining

In this phase, as they come out of blame, parents struggle to regain control of the reality that seems to have slipped away. They negotiate—but still cannot accept that their little one is "one of those."

- "I won't ask you anything about your life, and I don't want to know anything."
- "If you go to therapy, I'll pay."
- "You can still come over for Christmas, but come alone."
- "If you would go to church with me, I'll give you a car."
- "You sleep in the bedroom, and your *friend* sleeps on the couch."
- "Your *roommate* can join us for Thanksgiving but has to eat in the kitchen."

"Introductions are tricky in a lesbian relationship. It's a word game. To my friends she's my *lover*, to strangers and family members in denial she's my *roommate*, to Jehovah's Witnesses at the door she's my *lesbian sex slave*, and to my mother she's *Jewish* and that's all that matters."
—LESBIAN COMIC DENISE MCCANLES

You don't have to play this bargaining game with them. You don't have to defend yourself. I think it's best to find some humor in their attempts.

When my mother said, "You don't have to be in everyone's face," I so wanted to say, "You're right. I would rather be *on* everyone's face." I didn't say it, but just thinking of funny things helped me to deal with my parents' process.

Remember, you don't have to listen to parents' attempts to manipulate and control you. Love yourself and let them work it out. Because when you stop responding to their manipulations, they will give it up. Hey, if they persist on staying in this stage, next time they come over your house, make Mom and Dad sleep in separate beds. Sooner or later they'll move on to the next phase.

GET OFF THE CROSS, MOM, WE NEED THE WOOD!

Artist: Ann Glover © Judy Carter

© Donelan

"Oh, and Rick . . . your mother says to . . . huh . . . to bring your . . . huh . . . ow . . . to bring your . . . huh . . . your . . . Jeff."

Stage 6: Depression

Your parents see all their hopes and dreams crashing:

- **no big church wedding**
- **no grandchildren to spoil**
- **no photo albums of their doting daughter and son-in-law to impress their friends with**

- **no impressing *their* parents with what a catch their daughter/son got**

- **no validation that how they raised you was "right"**

They give up. It's hopeless. Their little pumpkin is a homo.

And all of a sudden your sexual orientation becomes *their* problem. They crash and have a pity party for one. "Poor me. What did I do to deserve this!" "How could you do this to me?" But hopefully they get bored with being depressed and realize how much they are missing out by not loving unconditionally. Perhaps your acceptance of them no matter how poorly they've been behaving will inspire them to take the next step.

Stage 7: Acceptance

Not tolerance, but true unconditional love. "We love and support you and accept who you are." They have let go of their idea of who they wanted you to be. They see you as a person separate from them. And perhaps they're really seeing you for the first time. They let go of their fears, doubts, and controls—and choose love. Congratulations, you and your lover have made it to their family photo album.

COMING OUT TO KIDS

I am a great believer in openness and complete honesty about being gay with children. I lived with my lover and her son, and we both parented her son from when he was thirteen years old until he left for college at eighteen. My lover was always honest with her son. When he was four years old, she heard him use the word *queer.* She then told him that Mommy is a lesbian, and some people call that being *queer,* and that's not nice. She kept explaining it to him as he got older: "Some people fall in love with men, and some with women. And Mommy falls in love with women." He grew up always knowing and thinking it was the most natural thing in the world, until the peer pressure days of his teenage years. In this sexually confusing passage, he became very aware of what others thought and didn't want his mother outing herself to his friends. We had very mixed feelings as we de-dyked the living room. Then, in college, he proudly outed himself as the son of a gay parent. We were so thrilled that he could come out and not feel that he had to hide. His process continues as he decides whom he feels comfortable to tell and whom he doesn't. Yet he has always respected that his mother never lied to him.

When a friend of mine, Vickie, came out as a lesbian at thirty-eight, it took her a year to be comfortable enough with her sexual orientation to come out to her children. Not telling them was out of the question because that would give the kids the message that there was something wrong and shameful with being gay. Deciding to talk to each kid separately, she found that her eight-year-old daughter and eleven-year-old son accepted their mother's sexual orientation without judgment. Her fourteen-year-old son had already guessed what was going on, and although he was relieved to talk about it, he was frightened about what his friends would think. She assured him that she would never out herself to his friends. She advised him that if anyone ever asked him if his mother was gay, he could simply joke and say, "Why? Does your mother want to date her?"

Hiding your sexual orientation gives children a negative and shameful example of sexuality. Hiding says to them:

"This is your Uncle Bobby's friend du jour."

- "I disapprove of myself."

- "I am ashamed of who I am."

- "You can't be who you are in this world."

- "You need to give up who you are in order to be a parent."

- "I don't trust you."

- "You have to keep secrets even from those you love."

If you are not out with your parents because you don't think they can handle it, and you are not out with your children, then aren't you continuing the legacy of secrets and mistrust? Homophobia—2. Love, trust, and communication—0. Come out and be a living example of having pride in yourself.

TIPS ON COMING OUT TO KIDS

- **Be open and honest, and talk with your heart.**

- **Let them know that you are not going to out them as kids of gays.**

- **Let them know that it's not something inherited, and just because *you* are gay, it doesn't mean that *they* are.**

- **Give them books to read. (Check the Appendix for a listing of books.)**

- **Join a support group such as Gay Parents. Or suggest that the kids go to a meeting of Children of Gays and Lesbians.**

- **Encourage them to talk about their worries, and assist them to work out solutions.**

- **Let them know of other kids who are in the same situation.**

- **Give them support as they go through their own coming-to-terms process.**

- **Give them time to cope.**

COMING OUT TO YOUR SPOUSE

It amazes me that some married people think that having affairs with same-sex partners is not cheating on their spouse. That's like thinking you haven't broken your diet if you eat ice cream with a fork.

- **"If I have sex standing up with a guy, that isn't cheating on my wife."**

- **"I didn't sleep over."**

- **"Sure I fucked, but I didn't kiss anyone."**

- **"There was no penetration, so that's not cheating."**

- **"I didn't take my shirt off."**

Isn't it interesting that some of us are so affected by homophobia that we diminish gay sex to the point where it doesn't even count as *real sex?*

There's Sally, a Houston housewife, who at thirty-eight realizes that she has "those" feelings for women. Her husband thinks she's at the church picnic, when actually she's at the women's bookstore. Her husband thinks she's out grocery shopping, when she's in bed with Kate, the grocer. She doesn't tell her husband because she is frightened to lose her financial security, her friends, her children.

There's Sam, who is online hot-chatting late night with "Hot Rod," while his wife is asleep. He is too frightened to tell his wife because he has convinced himself that he will lose his family, his job, his status.

When our coming out means hurting someone else, the consequences of being honest seem more severe.

If I come out I will lose . . .

- **my spouse**
- **my position in the community**
- **our friends**
- **my family**

So many gay people confine themselves to leading deceptive, double lives because they don't want to hurt anybody. But if you are using your marriage as an excuse for not coming out—well, who was it that said, "I do," in the first place? Perhaps you created this situation just so you could have an excuse not to be who you are.

Early Signs of Lesbianism

JOURNAL WORKSHOP: Coming Out to Your Spouse
Answer the following questions in your coming-out journal:

1. **Why did you really get married?**

2. **Why are you lying to your spouse?**

3. What is the worst that can happen if you come out?

4. What good can come from coming out?

5. How is your fear of hurting another keeping you from being who you are?

6. How much of your life are you living for others?

7. How does your relationship with your spouse parallel your relationship with your parents?

OTHER FAMILY OUTINGS: "DO I REALLY NEED TO TELL GRANDMA?"

It's interesting how so many of us stereotype older people as being less likely to accept our gayness. Yet my survey revealed that older people seem to be more accepting in many cases than one's parents. Maybe it's that they have lived longer and have mellowed. My friend's grandfather said, "It makes no difference to me. Some people like oranges and some people like apples."

My ultrareligious aunt Edith said, "As long as you are still the loving person you always were, what difference does it make?"—although she never quite understood when I told her about the book I was writing. "Coming out? Where are you going?"

STRETCH: Come Out, Come Out to Everyone

1. Make a list of all relatives you are not out to.

2. Put a star next to the relatives you're frightened to come out to.

3. Set a date that you can commit to and come out.

4. Do it!

Now that you've cleaned out your closets at home, it's 8 A.M. Let's go to work, you big queer!

Step 8: Come Out at Work

"We're here . . . We're queer . . . We're head of personnel!"

Is it safe for you to come out at work? Do you work for

- **Lesbian Avengers?**

- **ACT UP?**

- **Fernando's Beauty Salon?**

- **Judy Carter?**

- **U.S. Congressman Barney Frank?**

If you do, then chances are you're okay. In fact, at some places it's not safe to be *straight!*

Imagine if being straight could cost you your job . . .

Guys . . .

- **If they catch you with a picture of a woman on your desk, explain it came with the frame.**

- **Drop by a few gay bars after work to *network* with the boys.**

- **You'd better laugh at those breeder jokes. Otherwise they might think you're one of "them."**

- **If you are married, call your wife your roommate not to arouse suspicion.**

- **Practice saying, "Oh, yes! Yanni, what a talent!"**

Gals . . .

- **Hide your engagement ring. If they find out you're getting married to a *man*, it could cost you your job.**

- **Find a lesbian who can pretend to be your lover so you'll get medical benefits.**

- **At the Christmas party, bring a lesbian and learn how to lead.**

- **Don't wear panty hose or heels, no matter how good you feel in them. Wear sensible shoes so no one will talk.**

IMPOSSIBLE, DOC! COMING OUT WOULD END MY CAREER — KASPLAT! BLOOEY! POW! JUST LIKE THAT!

© Andrea Natalie

Everyone . . .

Above all, be very careful about whom you tell that you are straight. Try and find other straight people, but it will be hard because everyone will be trying to act gay. Use your "straightdar." Have faith. You're not the only one.

For many gays who are out everywhere else, work may remain the one place that they don't want to mess with. Okay, if you come out to your parents and it doesn't work out, you can move, but with work, you've got to be there Monday morning—that is, if you're not fired before Monday morning comes around.

In this chapter I'm going to ask you to . . .

- **examine how many of your fears about coming out at work are realistic and how many are imagined**

- **explore the negative effects of being in the corporate closet**

- **consider the positive aspects of coming out at work**

- **be open to the possibility of changing your work environment rather than conforming to it**

- **consider the possibility of coming out at work**

COMING OUT AT WORK—NOT FOR THE TIMID

....

For many of the gay people interviewed for this book, the possible repercussions of coming out at work were too great to make it a risk worth taking.

Fears

If I come out at work . . .

- I'll be fired. Here's a chant: "You're queer, you're outta here!"
- I'll be forced to look at their disapproval every day.
- I'll be treated differently by management.
- I'll be passed over for promotion.
- My career opportunities will be limited.
- I'll be stereotyped.
- I'll be snubbed by coworkers.
- I'll be the butt of jokes. "Sure, you'll bend over for a promotion. *Ha ha.*"
- I won't be able to work with children.
- Other closeted gays will abandon me so they're not "guilty by association."

If you want excuses to stay in the closet at work, many surveys can confirm your worst fears. According to a 1993 study done by the Los Angeles County Bar Association Committee on Sexual Orientation Bias . . .

- Fifty percent of L.A. attorneys believe that their work environment is less hospitable to gays than to heteros. They have witnessed antigay comments and jokes, as well as stereotyping of gay men as effeminate and HIV infected, of lesbians as unattractive and aggressive, and of both as unstable, uncontrolled sexually, or even criminally inclined.
- One in seven attorneys reports that their employer engages in antigay discrimination in the recruitment and hiring of workers.
- One in six attorneys reports that their employer engages in some form of sexual-orientation discrimination in work evaluation, promotion, and advancement, and that there is a glass ceiling for gays.
- Incomes for gay attorneys are substantially lower than for their heterosexual peers.

- **Most employers do not provide gays with employee benefits comparable to those provided to married heterosexuals.**

- **Despite the pain and isolation hiding can cause, many employers exert pressure on gay attorneys to remain in the closet.**

- **Gays encounter severe problems when it comes to networking.**

- **Same-sex couples are consciously or unconsciously excluded from many office-sponsored social events. There is a biased double standard against gays: while few gays would see the social introduction of an opposite-sex spouse or domestic partner as any sort of sexual statement, many heteros view the mention or social introduction of a same-sex domestic partner as inappropriate flaunting of one's sexuality.**

- **Employees perceived as being gay were fired and given vague reasons such as, "You don't fit in," or, "You're not a team player."**

The study concluded by saying that gays suffer from the same sexist thinking that in the past has eliminated women from the workplace or placed them in positions of inferiority. In the patriarchal, primarily white business world, manly qualities are considered good and female qualities bad.

Oddly enough, several attorneys commented that the common stereotype of lesbians as aggressive or macho is less of a problem and perhaps even a benefit in the practice of law. One lesbian attorney stated, "As a lesbian I was sexually harassed less than heterosexual women. I wasn't flirted with and didn't have

Sometimes when you come out at work—stereotyped

to flirt back, which was extremely helpful to me. Also, I was perceived a being more assertive or aggressive—as were the other lesbians—than the hetero women. So, we were given opportunities which heterosexual women were not."

Looking over coming-out horror stories, gay bias reports, and what's going on in the work environment, it's no wonder so many of us gays believe that hiding in the closet is the most certain and, in some instances, the only path to job security. And if coming out is career suicide, the consequences of staying in the closet are no picnic either. Some of the gay people I interviewed for this book had this to say:

"Not being out, I am anxious at every moment, trying to figure out whether and when I can say 'we' and risk someone asking who 'we' is. If someone asks, 'What happened this weekend?' and I slip and say 'we' instead of 'I,' then I go through a kind of turmoil. That really requires energy and prevents me from achieving any peace and assurance."

"I didn't want to partake in any of the sexist or antigay jokes that were being made in the groups who would gather to socialize in the office. But in removing myself from those situations, I got the reputation of being aloof. When I did speak up, I was seen as a malcontent, a troublemaker."

"It is exhausting having to be so aware of who calls me on the telephone. Closing the door when talking to my partner because someone might hear me use the word *honey*. It isolates me having to curtail the amount of time I interact with coworkers, because it's inevitable they ask, 'Are you seeing anyone?'"

"Not being out affected my potential because people began to experience me as indifferent or not a team player, and that showed up in my job performance report and my salary."

JOURNAL WORKSHOP: What If You Came Out at Work?

1. Make a list of the possible consequences of coming out at work. *If I come out at work . . .*

1. _____

2. _____

3. _____

4. _____

5. _____

6. _____

7. _____

8. _____

9. _____

10. _____

2. Let's examine your fears of coming out at work by doing the same fear exercise you did when coming out to your parents.

Are your fears about coming out at work realistic or imagined? Do this next exercise by putting one of your excuses into *A*. Then let yourself imagine where it goes.

If I come out at work, _____*A*_____ will happen.

If ____*A*____ happens, then _____*B*_____ will happen.

If ____*B*____ happens, then ____*C*____ will happen.

If ____*C*____ happens, then _____*D*_____ will happen . . .

For instance:

If I come out at work, *I'll get fired.*

If I get fired, *then I won't have any money.*

If I don't have any money, *I'll lose my home.*

If I lose my home, *I'll have to live on the streets.*

If I live on the streets, *I'll lose all my self-respect.*

If I lose all my self-respect, *life won't be worth living.*

If life is not worth living, *I'll kill myself.*

Do this exercise with all of your excuses. Don't censor yourself, but really let yourself run with it. Say the first thing that comes into your mind, no matter how stupid it sounds.

3. Now look over your list of fears and determine how many of them are realistic and how many are escalated fears. Can coming out at work really kill?

4. What are some *negative* consequences of staying in the closet?

1. _____
2. _____
3. _____
4. _____
5. _____
6. _____
7. _____
8. _____
9. _____
10. _____

5. Make a list of some *positive* repercussions of coming out at work.

1. _____
2. _____
3. _____
4. _____
5. _____
6. _____
7. _____
8. _____
9. _____
10. _____

WHY COME OUT?

Given all the horror stories and hardships involved with being out in corporate America, why *do* some gays come out? And why are so many of them successful?

- Why is Karen Lash, an out lesbian lawyer, dean of the conservative USC Law School?

- If gays are perceived as dangerous to children, why is Laura Lockner, an out lesbian, principal of an elementary school?

- If Hollywood is homophobic, why is David Geffen, an openly gay man, one of the most powerful movers and shakers in Hollywood?

- If the public is so supportive of a narrow definition of *family values*, why did Teri Schwartz, who was outed during her campaign for California Superior Court judge, win the election?

- If the music business is so homophobic, why is Melissa Etheridge out?

- If corporate America is so homophobic, why are huge successful companies such as Microsoft, Levi Strauss, Viacom, Ben & Jerry's, Lotus, Apple Computer, Time Warner, and MCA so gay friendly?

- If the world of publishing is so homophobic, why is the editor of this book, Chuck Adams, an out gay man?

So, why do some people get to come out at work with little or no negative consequences? Are they just lucky? What is it?

I have found that people who come out have these things in common:

- They were uncomfortable *not* being themselves in *all* areas of their lives.

- They were willing to suffer coming-out consequences.

- Their personal comfort level was as important as job security.

- They were uncomfortable with lying about their sexual orientation.

- They realized that they can create a positive work environment by coming out.

- They were able to enroll the support of their heterosexual coworkers.

- They were open to educating their companies on the effects of homophobia in the workplace.

- They had a positive attitude about being gay.

Karen Lash, dean of USC Law School, was out while interviewing for jobs right at the get-go. As she told me, "I put on my résumé, 'Gay and Lesbian Law Union.' Being out has actually helped me in my career. I got a very prestigious

position working for a federal judge who was a Carter appointee. He thought, 'This is great. I never hired an out lesbian or a gay person before.' The same thing with other progressive groups; having an out lesbian was beneficial for them. Some liberal firms are now embarrassed if they don't have an openly gay employee."

Jon Henderson, program manager in the Developer Division at Microsoft, said:

"When I started at Microsoft, they moved both me and my partner up there, paying for everything and helping him find a job. Nobody seems to have batted an eye over anything! Matter of fact, the recruiter, upon offering me the job, asked, 'Can I send your lover a bottle of wine or some flowers to help you make your decision?'"

Kathryn Rivers, manager at Kodak in Rochester, New York, said:

"I initially turned down a management position because, although it would mean more income, I was in the closet, and it meant more visibility, and that was too scary. When I finally told my boss that I was gay, he was very supportive. We have *both* gone through a process of feeling more comfortable about my sexual orientation, and I've since been promoted to management and have become active in Lambda, with the full support of my company in initiating nondiscrimination training seminars."

According to David Frishkorn, Xerox manager,

"I find that the relief and joy of being open and honest far outlasts the advantages of not being out. Xerox has a benchmark Valuing Diversity program, including training for

managers and new employers, showing how all employees need to be respected whether they be African American, disabled, Latino, or gay. When a manager at Xerox was reported to have made homophobic remarks, the company required him not to *take* the diversity-training workshops but to *give* them."

No matter what you've read about homophobic corporate America, most of the people interviewed for this book who did come out at work expressed freedom and little regret, even if they lost their job.

- **"My sexuality was no longer my problem, but became their problem."**
- **"Coming out at a hostile company made me realize that work didn't need to be so difficult, and I got a better job at a gay-friendly company."**
- **"It's just one big relief. Now I can have my lover's picture on my desk and get to show my coworkers my vacation pictures!"**

"Interesting résumé . . . Do you really consider shopping a hobby?"

- **"I've become part of the solution to better understanding between straights and gays."**
- **"I've become an activist initiating nondiscrimination policies at my company."**
- **"Now they are afraid to fire me, because I've come out as a lesbian, and even though I'm bad at my job, they're afraid of a sexual-orientation lawsuit. Ha ha!"**

IF COMING OUT AT WORK IS SO LIBERATING, WHY DOESN'T EVERYONE DO IT?

When the pain of being in the closet is greater than the pain of losing your job, you will probably come out.

Basically, for those who come out at work, it stopped working for them *not* to be out. Their belief system told them that "it's okay to be who I am," even if their boss told them differently. Some of them had the benefit of being brought up in families where they received total acceptance, even though they were different. And some of them launched themselves on a growth path that brought them to believe that the consequences of lying are more damaging than the consequences of telling the truth.

Some workers will never feel safe enough to come out, and that's okay. Nobody can force another person to risk. Coming out is a very personal choice. It's an opportunity to be courageous, and no one should rob another person of that opportunity by outing them. But whether you choose to come out at work or not, take a moment to examine which of your beliefs are keeping you in the closet when, in the long run, it might be to your advantage to come out.

TEST: WHAT IS YOUR BELIEF SYSTEM TELLING YOU?

Check those which are true for you.

❑ I believe that I can't make a living if I am out.

❑ I believe that my security comes from having my current job.

❑ Work is not supposed to be fun or enjoyable. It's a grind, and lying about my sexuality is just a part of it.

❑ I don't believe in taking risks with my job.

❑ Being gay is looked on negatively in corporate America.

❑ I believe I can't come out because I work at a company that is very gay unfriendly.

❑ I believe that being honest is worth all the consequences.

❑ I believe that lying is bad no matter what the consequences.

❑ I believe that my sexual orientation will not affect my job.

❑ I believe that taking risks does not ultimately affect my security.

❑ I believe that I can find a job where I can be who I am.

❑ I believe that if I'm fired for being gay, it wasn't the right job.

❑ I believe that my security is based on my feelings about myself, not my job.

❑ I believe that lying about my personal life affects all areas of my life.

❑ I believe that the job I have now is the best I can get.

❑ I'm too old to change jobs.

- ❏ I believe that if I come out, I'll be ghettoized into a gay market.

- ❏ I believe that if I come out at work, I will be passed over for promotion.

- ❏ I believe that this job is the only way to get health insurance.

- ❏ I think that straight coworkers won't like me if they know I'm gay.

- ❏ I don't believe that not being out has any effect on me.

We can't always change our beliefs, but we can become aware of them and how they affect our lives. And if some of your beliefs are holding you back, you might want to really take some time to examine them further. Looking over what you checked will give you a good idea of why you are in the situation you find yourself in. Our beliefs create our personal reality, and there is also a communal reality created by everyone. So if 10 percent of the workforce is gay and only a small percentage of gays are out, then it's no wonder that corporate America is such a homophobic place. Who created that situation? We all did—straights and gays.

Everything in our lives is a result of what we believe, and we all have beliefs, most of them unconscious, about everything. If you believe that "jobs are security," then it's no wonder that you wouldn't do anything to disturb that security. But are your beliefs really true, or do they just become valid because you believe in them? For instance . . .

"My job is my security."

Of course, when you've got rent to pay, food to buy, and perhaps no savings, money can appear to be security. But does work really provide security? Is your current job your only source of money? Is what the company's giving you equal to what you are giving it?

It used to be that a worker could depend on working for one company for her or his entire lifetime and expect to be provided with a decent salary, retirement, pension, and medical benefits. But now, with layoffs, corporate downsizing, union busting, and bankrupt pension funds, workers no longer have job security. Now it is very typical for people to have many different jobs during their lifetime. This has created a feeling of panic in the workplace, and not only among gays.

Are you selling yourself short by trading the truth of who you are for a job that might not be there, no matter what you do? Perhaps you are putting too much of your conviction in your work, and not enough in yourself.

"The biggest mistake you can make is to believe that you are working for someone else."
—ANONYMOUS

"Work is not supposed to be fun or enjoyable. It's a grind."

Are you cutting yourself short by staying at a job that you don't like? Why are there so many out gays who earn plenty of money doing what they love to do? Could it be that they have a different belief about work than you? Can you imagine getting paid for something you enjoy doing?

"I don't believe in taking risks with my job."

It's interesting that some people don't consider taking risks at work, and yet stories about successful companies always have at their core a risk taker. People who bucked the status quo created Apple, Microsoft, Snowboards, Rollerblades . . . and on and on. Competing in today's market means hiring innovators, not firing them.

Perhaps taking a risk and coming out will unleash your creative energy.

"Being gay is looked on negatively in corporate America."

In some companies this statement is absolutely true. But many companies not only are gay friendly but actively recruit gays who are out. Given that the gay community is perceived as a huge income source, many companies are cognizant of the benefits of having openly gay employees.

Life experiences of gays and lesbians have caused many of us to develop skills that are useful in business. We tend to become more diplomatic, conciliatory, accepting of cultural diversity, and even more creative in problem-solving. Not all of us possess such skills, but our life experiences incline us to develop these skills to a greater degree than the majority of straights.

Many biotech firms show a gay orientation when hiring public relations people and clinical-trial experts for testing AIDS drugs. Many marketing firms, recognizing the extremely high brand-name loyalty of gays to gay-friendly products, hire gays almost exclusively for these accounts. And other companies hire gays simply because they want a more *representative* workforce; their perception is that a workforce in tune with society at large will be better capable of producing products that match the population's desires. And the majority of companies just don't give a damn about a worker's sexual, racial, or gender orientation.

A hiring manager said, "The more comfortable my workforce is, the more productive they will be. And this means that they must perceive themselves as able to be themselves when on the job. Homophobia, heterosexism, and racial tensions only cause problems for a diverse workforce."

As another corporate executive so eloquently said, "I don't care if my employees are fucking a donkey, as long as they get the work done."

Coming out can transform negatives into positives.

"I can't come out because I work at a company that is very gay unfriendly."

And who got you that job? You did. Is it possible that you are in your current job, no matter how hostile it is, because on a subconscious level you are recreating the environment of your childhood family?

"Why would I want to recreate my family environment?" you might say. "I hated it. I moved away to be free of them. Why would I do that?"

Perhaps we get ourselves into situations because they are familiar. Our work environment might be painful, unpleasant, and exasperating, but if that's what our childhood was like, then a kind, loving environment where we are totally accepted might be too strange.

"I like earthquakes because they bring back all those warm fuzzy, familiar feelings of childhood. Glass shattering, people screaming . . . 'Daddy's home!'"
—COMIC ADAM DRUCKER

"When I get home I'll explain the difference between out and outrageous . . . again!"

For so long I had lied onstage, talking about a fictitious "boyfriend," because I believed that if I came out, I wouldn't work. Yet since coming out I have had more work than I can handle and have tripled my income. The real reason I didn't come out wasn't money. It was that I had bought into the belief my parents taught me: "If you are yourself, you won't be loved."

Before coming out, it's important to become conscious of all of your beliefs. Do the following journal exercises with an open mind and you might be surprised at some of the similarities between your family and your work.

JOURNAL WORKSHOP: "Dad . . . oh, I mean boss!"

1. What similarities do you find between your work environment and your family?

2. If you feel excluded at work, did you feel excluded in your family?

3. Do you have a dynamic with your boss similar to what you had with your father? With your mother?

COMING OUT AT WORK—PRACTICAL ADVICE

• Find out what your rights are. As of the printing of this book, only eight states have a nondiscrimination policy toward gays. And although many companies have a nondiscrimination policy, it means nothing unless it can be enforced.

• Find others who have come out and talk with them to get a feel for what you can expect.

• Get advice from your company's gay and lesbian support group, if there is one.

• If you truly feel you might be fired, have economical alternatives lined up to last you while you find a new job.

• When looking for a job, research and find employment at gay-friendly companies. Some indications of progressive companies are that they have a lot of female partners, offer child care, and show ethnic diversity in management. Check in the Appendix of this book for listings of resource books and organizations that can assist you in finding gay-friendly companies.

• If you are currently looking for a job, you can avoid an unfriendly work environment through coming out on your résumé by listing any memberships in prestigious gay organizations such as Lambda and GLAAD, or local gay groups.

COME OUT AT WORK BY BEING YOURSELF

Coming out at work doesn't mean making a big declarative speech. Coming out at work can be as simple as putting a picture of your lover on your desk. Or . . .

- **When a coworker tries to fix you up and says, "I'd like you to meet my sister," reply: "Well, thank you, but being gay, chances are I would be more interested in your brother."**

- **If you are in a committed relationship, start wearing your wedding band at work. People asked a lesbian friend what her husband did. She simply said with a smile, "*She* works for a pharmacy."**

- **Put pictures of your lover on your desk right next to your "I can't even *think* straight" coffee mug.**

- **Participate in complaining about your relationship, just like everyone else. "After everything I've done for him (her), I never get flowers."**

- **Show your coworkers your vacation pictures.**

- **Make it known that antigay jokes are inappropriate because you're gay. Many people who tell those horrible jokes are not really homophobic but ignorant and insensitive. You might be the first person who ever told them that antigay statements are not funny but hurtful, not only to gay workers but to all the employees who have gay family members. Or segue into your own jokes: "Okay, two heteros walk into a bar and put on really bad music . . ."**

- **Have a private conversation with your boss.**

COMING OUT TO YOUR BOSS

If you come out at work in a subtle way, you might want to take the time to educate your boss about your sexual orientation. Remember, homophobia has been everyone's teacher, and it's up to us to reeducate those people who can have a direct effect on our lives. You might want to explain to your boss that *being out means* . . .

- **"I can be a better employee because I'm not using all my energy to hide."**

- **"I won't be flaunting my sexuality, just not lying about it."**

- **"I will be able to participate more with coworkers and in company events."**
- **"I will be more at ease knowing that my company supports a nondiscrimination policy for all people."**
- **"You don't have to agree with or like my sexual orientation. I just don't want to be discriminated against because of it."**
- **"I won't be fired for something I can't change."**

"Hoo boy! Check out the boobs on that one!"

- **"Creating an even playing field, where I can achieve according to my skills, not my sexual orientation."**
- **"Letting others know that homophobic jokes are inappropriate in the workplace."**
- **"Creating a workplace where diversity is valued."**
- **"I'm *not* going to be in everyone's face with it."**

Most important, ask your boss what his or her concerns are about your being out, and really listen. If your company perceives its clients as ultraconservative, they might think that your being openly gay would not be in line with company image. Tell your boss that you know that in business not everyone needs to know. It's not that you hide who you are; you just don't need to tell everyone. Your boss needs to know this because, although he or she doesn't have a problem with your sexual orientation, his or her worst fantasy might be that you are going to be in the client's face. "Hello, thank you for opening your account with us. And oh, by the way, I'm a big homo."

WHAT IF YOU GET FIRED?

If you are fired for being gay, your coming out can wake up the world if you file a sexual-orientation-discrimination lawsuit (or at least get on *Hard Copy*). As more and more courts are ruling on behalf of gay people, companies are beginning to take sexual-orientation bias very seriously. It used to be status quo for men to make sexist comments and sexually harass women. But then Texaco lost millions of dollars in one of the first sexual harassment cases, and Anita Hill put the issue under closer scrutiny, and sexual harassment became too costly for companies to tolerate. The same is starting to happen for gays.

Unfortunately, it's still pretty easy for employers to fire gay people and make it appear to be about something else. If you want to file a sexual-orientation-discrimination lawsuit, you will need to have evidence of sexual-orientation bias, namely witnesses, tape recordings, and other documentation. You can get legal advice from one of the organizations listed in the Appendix.

Change starts with us, and until we no longer accept oppression but fervently and actively resist it, we will be oppressed. We have got to stand tall and not allow ourselves to be made or perceived as less. And this extends far beyond the employment context. This applies with everyone.

Read on . . .

Step 9: Become a Bigot Basher

"Let us spread the idea of tolerance by practicing it ourselves, even toward bigots."
—LEE CROCKER

You're a together homo. You're out almost everywhere. You feel that lavender glow as you dance on that float in the gay pride parade. And judging by the rainbow decal on your car, plus the fourteen other bumper stickers declaring your

TOP TEN REASONS WHY BIG BERTHA CREATED BIGOTS

1. To give us the right to question Darwinism.
2. To fill daytime talk shows.
3. To challenge just how out we are.
4. Because Big Bertha had bodies left over, but not enough brains to go around.
5. As a gift to gay stand-up comics.
6. To supply a market for fried pork rinds.
7. To give us a reason to live near a coast.
8. To demonstrate the starting point of evolution.
9. Because someone has to go to tractor pulls.
10. To inspire us to have tolerance for people who are different from us.

preferences and allegiances, someone would have to be mentally retarded not to know you're queer. Oh, you're so confident, you've quit therapy. "I'm queer, I'm here, I'm fabulous!"

And just when you're feeling like a proud little homo, along comes this one person, this right wing, tobacco-chewing, redneck, white trash, trailer-park, dumb-ass, Wal-Mart-shoppin' bigot that throws you for a loop. It can be someone sitting across from you on Thanksgiving at your parents' house. It can be a stranger on a bus. It can be a coworker eating lunch next to you in the cafeteria. Whoever. You hear the words *faggots! . . . dykes!*

And for some reason this person scares you and you don't say anything. The score: bigot—1; homo—0.

Coming out to someone we know will disagree with, even hate, us is our constant challenge. We can choose to hate them or we can choose to see them as gifts. Okay, not the kind of thing we hope to receive on our birthday, or at Christmas or Hanukkah, but a gift nonetheless.

Bigots are gifts because they are forever creating another opportunity for us to choose love and pride over hate and shame and to grow in our own humanness. Perhaps there is a synchronicity to our paths crossing with one of these people. When something comes into your life the exact moment you're ready for it, perhaps it isn't a coincidence. Maybe it's an event that you created yourself to give yourself another coming-out challenge. Either that or you live in Utah.

JOURNAL WORKSHOP: **Bigot Confrontations**

What happens when you are confronted with a bigot?

1. **In the past month, did you *not* come out to someone because it felt dangerous to do so?**

2. **What was it about that person that made you hold your tongue?**

3. **What were you frightened of happening if you came out to her or him?**

4. **How did it feel not to come out to that person?**

Being gay may not be about choice, but coming out is. In coming out to big-ots it's important to know the difference between your homophobic aunt Bee and a gang of skinheads. Chances are your aunt Bee doesn't have a tire chain in her pants and razor blades in the toes of her shoes. Sometimes it's a real good choice to hold your tongue when someone else is holding a gun.

WHEN *NOT* TO COME OUT

- **When it's not a barbecue but a cross burning, and the only weenie they are going to roast is yours.**
- **When people are wearing white hats that come to a point, and it's not Halloween.**
- **When there is one of you and a truckful of beer-drinking seven-teen-year-olds with a bumper sticker that says, "People kill peo-ple, not guns!"**
- **When you're around any postal worker.**
- **When you're waiting in line for Rush Limbaugh tickets.**

DIFFERENT KINDS OF BIGOTS

Bigots generally fall into two groups: violent and nonviolent. But be warned, they both can cause a lot of damage if you're not careful.

Violent, Gay-Bashing Bigots

These are usually young men with more testosterone than brains. These are people who consider bashing a "fag" or a "dyke" their initiation into manhood. They travel in packs and have SAT scores equal to their age. There is nothing you can say or do to change them, short of frontal lobotomy.

Basically, the only way to deal

The Quintessential Bigot

Artist: Donelan © Judy Carter

with these idiots is on a political level, not one-on-one. Give your money to pro-gay PACs such as the ACLU, Lambda, the National Gay and Lesbian Task Force, GLAAD, or the other organizations listed in the Appendix of this book. These organizations are working to create laws to protect against gay bashing and educate the police and the public on the issues. Violent, gay-bashing jerks may have guns, but you have a pen.

"Now that it is increasingly clear that HIV can be transmitted to heterosexuals . . . the self-righteous must find another reason for gay bashing."
—BISHOP DESMOND TUTU

Nonviolent Bigots

These bigots are everywhere—in your church, at work, and in your family. Some of these bigots are homophobic and some are just ignorant. If some of these big-ots truly knew the effect that their words had, they might stop.

Take for example the story that appeared on the *20/20* TV show about a farmer in the Midwest who was homophobic and didn't know that his brother was gay. The brother had led a very secretive life until his shame about being gay was so great that he hanged himself. His brother was devastated and came too late to realize that his offhanded remarks about gays contributed to his beloved brother's death. He had a huge realization of how he had become a product of homophobia and how homophobia truly kills. As he became ac-countable, this self-professed redneck farmer became an activist for gays. He now crosses the country speaking at churches, spreading his message of love and acceptance.

"Jerry Falwell is so homophobic that he quit the church he was going to because the choir insisted on singing 'Go Down, Moses.'"
—COMIC AND PRODUCER ROBIN TYLER

Do not underestimate the negative force of homophobia. It's so all-pervasive and subtle that it seeps into the psyches of even card-carrying members of the ACLU, liberals, Democrats, prochoicers, the NAACP, feminists, and, unfortu-nately, other homos.

Corporate Bigots

Homophobia affects company policy. They don't want to hire, work with, or pro-mote homos. Sometimes it's subtle: "You just aren't a team player." And some-times it's overt: "You're fired, you big homo!" Yet there is hope as more people come out and more companies make homophobic behavior unacceptable. Let's face it, the people who tell fag and dyke jokes today are the same kind of insensitive people who ten years ago were discriminating blatantly against women. They just need to be told clearly and repeatedly—as they have about sex discrimination—that it is not acceptable behavior.

Liberal Bigots

Homophobic card-carrying members of the ACLU, NOW, and the Sierra Club. These people tend to

be more subtle about their feelings. In some ways these folks can be more dangerous because you don't know what you're dealing with. They contribute to liberal causes but don't invite their son's lover over on Thanksgiving. When confronted with their own homophobia, they generally turn as red as the AIDS ribbons they wear.

"The air force pinned a medal on me for killing a man and discharged me for making love to one."

—FORMER AIR FORCE SERGEANT LEONARD MATLOVICH (1943–1988), WHO IN 1975 SET HIMSELF UP AS A TEST CASE TO CHALLENGE THE U.S. MILITARY'S POLICY OF AUTOMATICALLY DISCHARGING HOMOSEXUALS

Gay Bigots

J. Edgar Hoover, Roy Cohn (Senator Joseph McCarthy's lawyer), gay U.S. generals (yes, there are some) who support the "Don't ask, don't tell" position, gay governors who veto gay rights bills. Don't be fooled. Many members of the anti-gay, right-wing Christian Coalition who are judging during the day have been seen cruising gay bars at night. One way or another, they are screwing us.

"If God dislikes gays so much, how come he picked Michelangelo, a known homosexual, to paint the Sistine Chapel ceiling while assigning Anita Bryant to go on TV and push orange juice?"

—CHICAGO COLUMNIST MIKE ROYKO

Religious Bigots

These are the self-righteous, holier-than-thou, Bible-totin' homophobic bigots. It's hard to enlighten someone who believes that they have the will of Big Bertha on their side. Maybe instead of carrying the Bible, they should read it and really try to understand it.

"You will never be rid of us because we produce ourselves out of your bodies."
—WRITER MARTHA SHELLEY

"Yes, Brother Fred, your cell is lovely . . . as a matter of fact that's why I'm here."

COMING-OUT-TO-BIGOTS TIPS

1. You don't have to change them—just don't let them change you.

2. Don't let them get to you by reacting to anger with anger.

3. Be out by being yourself. They're the ones that make the big deal about it.

4. Practice coming out to bigots on-line in CompuServe on Rush Limbaugh's forum or in Christianity On-line in America Online or in the many Internet sites. When on-line you can even eavesdrop without them knowing you are there. From listening you can get a really good idea of how these people think—or rather, don't think. When you feel ready, jump in. It's safe and fun, and because most chat lines use nicknames, it's totally anonymous.

   On CompuServe I entered the room where these dittoheads were gay bashing and announced that "there is a lesbian amongst you." They hit me pretty hard with their hostile rhetoric, but there was one person who, although holding similar antigay views, felt embarrassed by how hostile and harsh the "boys" were being to me. We began a private E-mail communication that lasted several months, and he actually came to believe that antigay sentiment was "inhuman and un-Christian." For a listing of BBS boards, check the Appendix.

Keep your sense of humor—this is the most powerful weapon you have, and it drives them crazy.

"Catholic girls make the best dykes because their whole lives they're told, 'Having sex with men is a sin!' 'Oh . . . okay.'"
—JUDY CARTER

BIGOT-BASHING COMEBACKS

....

- **Homosexuals are a cult. They'll just suck you in!**
  "Duh! That's why I joined."—Texas comic Vickie Shaw

- **They should take all the homosexuals and put them on an island.**
  "They did, and they call it Manhattan."—comic Robin Tyler.

- **God made penises and vaginas. It's impossible to be born homosexual. There's no such thing.**
  "God made brains too . . . and there are still stupid people."

- **You shouldn't hang around those kind of people. They will convert you before you convert them.**
  "The only thing that was convertible in the gay pride parade was the Mustang!"

- **You shouldn't hang around them because you might catch it.**
  "Well, it was either that or leprosy, and it would upset my boyfriend if my dick fell off."

- **If you were really spiritual, the feelings for the opposite sex would just come from the Holy Spirit.**
  "If you were really spiritual, love and compassion would just come from the Holy Spirit. Funny how that works!"

- **God is perfect. Why would he make such a big mistake ten percent of the time?**

  "Maybe because it's not a mistake. And it's more like twenty-five percent!"

- **So—with this homosexuality, do you think you are fornicating?**

  "Well, with this heterosexuality, do you think you are judging? 'Judge not lest ye be judged.'"

- **I love the sinner. I just hate the sin.**

  "Do you really love *me?* Then don't fire me from my job, don't take away my constitutional rights, don't take my children away from me, don't murder me . . . That is . . . if you love *me."*

- **All homosexuals are going to hell.**

  "Heaven is going to be one big drag with people like you in it. And I bet the music will suck."

  "If there aren't going to be gays in heaven, I'd like to know where you are going to get your hair done. Heaven is going to be one bad hair day after the next!"

  "So, people like Michelangelo; Leonardo da Vinci; James I of England, who commissioned the King James translation of the Bible; Mary queen of Scotland, England, and Ireland; and my homosexual brothers and sisters with the gifts of compassion, faith, love, and understanding are going to hell. And people who judge, hate, kill, and despise are going to heaven. Help me on this one . . . where do I want to go?"

Q: Dear Abby: A pair of gay men is moving in across the street. What can we do to improve the neighborhood?

A: You could move.

—ABIGAIL VAN BUREN

- **The Bible says, "If a man lies with a man as one lies with a woman . . . he must be put to death"—Leviticus 20:13.**

  "Yes, but what a way to go."

  "Yes, and that's why I'm a lesbian."

  It also says in the Bible that "he who touches a pig must be put to death," and also that "he who wears clothing woven of two kinds of materials shall be put to death." So if you want to be literal, no more NFL (touching pigskin = death) and no more poly-cotton blends. And it wasn't us gays who invented polyester!"

- **Gays recruit children.**

  "I'd worry more about all the straight people who molest them."

"Since both my parents are straight, it seems as if heteros are doing all the recruiting."

- **We have to do something about the gay agenda.**

"Do you have a copy of it, because when I signed up for being gay, I didn't get a copy. My recruiter said it was in the mail, but I never got it!"

"Wouldn't it be great if you could only get AIDS from giving money to television preachers?"
—COMEDIENNE ELAYNE BOOSLER

- **You can't be gay and be a Christian.**

"I'm sorry, I must have a misprint in my Bible . . . I'll have to take it back. It doesn't say, 'For God so loved the world that he gave his only begotten son, that whosoever believeth in him, *except homosexuals*, should not perish but have everlasting life.'"

- **Homosexuals are already covered under the Constitution just like the rest of us. What they want are *special rights*. We oppose *special rights* for homosexuals.**

"If *special* means the right to get and keep a job based on merit, equal access to housing, renting a hotel room and being served food in a restaurant . . . if *special* means the right to have and raise children without the state seizing them, and the right to walk down a street and not get attacked because of who you are and whom you love . . . then you're right: I want the same special rights of all American citizens. And it looks as if you want the very special right to discriminate against those you hate. We call that 'special righteousness.'"

- **Local ordinances for gay men and lesbians force the rest of us to live against our religious beliefs. We're entitled to our rights too.**

"You can still have your right to hate, but we are entitled to our right to love."

- **Homosexuals have an abominable lifestyle. People who care about traditional family values must not encourage the open expression of this sexual depravity.**

"Since when are discrimination, hate, and bigotry traditional family values?"

"Family values! You must be talking about the Manson family . . . and they were straight."

"The family values we uphold are support, love, understanding, and respect."

But the bottom line to all of this is, "Big Bertha created me, so it can't be wrong."

STOP YOURSELF FROM BECOMING A BIGOT

If we truly do stop and examine ourselves, we might be shocked to find our own bigotry. Most everyone thinks of themselves as kind, loving, and unjudging. But if you think about it, that person who treated you horribly in your last relationship still thinks of her- or himself as a wonderful person. Look at the personals ads. Are there really that many people who are "sincere, attractive, and have a great sense of humor"? If you've ever responded to a personals ad, you know that people lie, lie, lie.

Guess what? The whole world is not living in self-deception except for you.

TEST: EXAMINING YOUR BIGOTRY

Check the categories of people you believe to be oppressed in some way.

❏ **African Americans**

❏ **Latinos**

❏ **women**

❏ **poor people**

❏ **children**

❏ **fat people**

❏ **single parents**

❏ **drag queens**

❏ **butch women**

❏ **others:**

_____

_____

_____

_____

_____

_____

How many of those people you've checked do you include in your life? How many do you let in? Or do you relax in your feeling of superiority? "Well, I might be gay, but I drive a BMW. I'm thin, young, and I'm not one of *them*."

As long as you judge yourself better than someone else, you are not. As long as you need to suppress others to feel a sense of worth, you have become a part of the problem, and that doesn't work. Even straights need your understanding, your empathy, your knowledge, and your love. Everyone will agree that the world needs love—that is, of course, if the other person makes the first move. Try going first.

STRETCH: Take a Bigot to Lunch

Throughout your coming-out process, you have asked people to tolerate you, accept you, and love you in spite of your differences. Can you love someone who is different? Forget about love—how about lunch? This next stretch is an eight-step process to resolve conflict. Try it.

Step 1: Acknowledge Who It Is You Dislike

Find someone who really gets to you. They might be someone who is ignorant, fat, different. They

"I'm just tired of people pinning labels on me . . . especially the yuppies and the rednecks."

might be that homophobic redneck who lives next door. Perhaps it is someone you have a major conflict or disagreement with. Write down some names here.

_____

_____

_____

_____

_____

_____

Step 2: Admit Your Own Prejudices

Pick one person from the above list and write down all your annoyances about that person or about certain aspects of that person. What about him or her really bugs you? What are your judgments about that person? What are your limiting beliefs? Don't worry here about being politically incorrect. "I can't stand to look at someone so fat." "He is such a fag." "This guy is so stupid." "I don't want anyone to see me with them." "He's a hopeless homophobe." Let it all out.

1. _____

2. _____

3. _____

4. _____

5. _____

6. _____

7. _____

8. _____

9. _____

10. _____

Step 3: Create Possibility

Write down some of the possibilities of your relationship. "We could be friendly toward each other." "We could have understanding of each other."

Don't stick to reality. Imagine the most positive kind of relationship.

A friend of mine had huge conflict with her landlord, who was trying to evict her because she was gay. She couldn't imagine any possibility of resolving her conflict, other than in court. But when she was pushed to really imagine what some *positive* possibilities of their relationship could be, she came up with: "We could live together without conflict." "We could stop threatening each other." And the unimaginable: "This dyke and this bigot could become friends."

Of course she thought becoming friends was not only highly unlikely but very undesirable. But after she went through this eight-step procedure, that is exactly what happened.

Write the possibilities here.

1. _____

2. _____

3. _____

4. _____

5. _____

6. _____

7. _____

8. _____

9. _____

10. _____

Step 4: Take Action

Initiate a conversation with this person and share with her or him your vision of the possibility of your relationship. "I want to talk to you because I think we can find things we have in common and become friends."

Step 5: Dig Out Their Concerns

Ask them what their upsets are, and really listen.

Step 6: Re-create Their Concerns Without Judgment

Mirror their concerns back to them without getting defensive. "So you think gay people are sinners? I get that." Once you repeat their concerns, dig out more. "Is there anything else?" This communication can sound like this . . .

Them: I think that you are an unfit mother because you are gay.
You: So you think because I'm gay I am not a good mother?
Them: Yes.
You: What else is upsetting you?
Them: I just don't like it. It makes me uncomfortable.
You: So me being gay makes you uncomfortable. I get that. Anything else?
Them: I think it's sick.
You: So you think I'm sick because I'm gay, right?
Them: Yes.
You: I get that you think that. Anything else?

Get the idea? Don't react. Don't get hooked into their drama.

Step 7: Repeat Your Vision

After you truly exhaust this person of all concerns and you've truly listened and re-created their concerns, transformation is possible. It is at this point that you can once again express your vision of a relationship with this person that is your vision of the world. "I still believe that despite our different beliefs, if we got to know each other, we could like each other."

Step 8: Open Yourself to Unimagined Possibilities

Don't be surprised if the other person shares a possibility you haven't even thought of. If you give another person an opportunity to really express his or her grievances, and if that person feels truly received and heard, in many cases the grievances will vanish. For when you open the space for another to be heard, you open up the possibility of change.

JOURNAL WORKSHOP: **We Are All Alike**

THE
HOMO
HANDBOOK

....

193

Have you ever wondered why these seemingly "bad" people are crossing your path? Perhaps there is a reason why you are drawing them to you. Take out your coming-out journal and answer these questions. After having your conversation with a bigot, answer the following questions in your coming-out journal:

1. **How does this person represent something or someone familiar?**

2. **How are you alike?**

3. **If you walked in their shoes, is it a possibility you would end up exactly like them?**

4. **If not, what opportunities did you have that they didn't?**

5. **Can you feel empathy for them?**

Be open to the fact that we can't control how people feel about us and that there are some very hard-core gay bashers that can't be dealt with one-on-one. That's why the next step is about becoming a gay activist. Gay bashers might travel in packs, but we've got PACs—political action committees. Read on . . .

Step 10: Become an Activist

"We know what happens to people who stay in the middle of the road. They get run over."
—BRITISH M.P. ANEURIN BEVAN

Are you fed up with the lies that others tell about us? Then become a part of the solution. Take gay-positive action by becoming an activist. Being an activist doesn't necessarily mean going to jail. There are all kinds of activism, from simply coming out to civil disobedience to wrapping bigots up in an electric blanket and pouring water on them.

Gay activism began dramatically in June 1969, when the patrons of the Stonewall Inn, a Greenwich Village gay bar, fought back against police violence during a raid. Since then hundreds of gay organizations have sprung up. Rather than being individuals struggling in isolation, by acting as a mass we have become powerful. In a relatively short period of time, gay activist groups have achieved significant progress in helping us gain equal rights under the law. According to the ACLU Gay and Lesbian Project . . .

- **sodomy laws that previously existed in all fifty states now exist in only twenty-three states**
- **eight states, the District of Columbia, and over a hundred municipalities now ban discrimination based on sexual orientation in employment, housing, and public accommodations**

• dozens of municipalities and many more private institutions, including some of the country's largest corporations and universities, have domestic partnership programs that recognize and grant various benefits, such as health insurance coverage, to gay and lesbian partners

But it's not enough. There's a lot of work to be done.

WHAT DO WE WANT?

• Repeal of sodomy laws by the legislatures and their invalidation by the courts, until such laws have been consigned to history in every state

• Protection against employment discrimination
  All existing federal civil rights laws must be amended to ban discrimination based on sexual orientation in employment, hous-

I'M SORRY, YOU CAN'T CLAIM THE TURKEY BASTER AS A SPOUSAL DEDUCTION.

IRS

DEDUCTION

Artist: Ann Glover © Judy Carter

ing, public accommodations, public facilities, and federally assisted programs. We want laws prohibiting discrimination on the basis of sexual orientation so that we will be judged according to our abilities, not our sexual orientation.

• Legalization of domestic partnerships
  We want all of the economic benefits accorded to married couples, such as sick and bereavement leave, insurance and survivorship benefits.

"Isn't it a violation of the Georgia sodomy law for the Supreme Court to have its head up its ass?"
—LETTER TO *PLAYBOY* MAGAZINE, FEBRUARY 1987

• Legalization of gay marriages
  Denying our relationships full legal recognition is a blatant reinforcement of our status as second-class citizens and deprives us of benefits that married heterosexuals take for granted. Married people automati-

cally enjoy certain tax advantages; they can inherit property from one another without a will; they can recover damages for the wrongful death of a spouse; they can adopt children more easily than singles can. Employers often extend health insurance, pension, and other benefits on the basis of marital status. Practically speaking, we cannot achieve complete equality in American society until the government officially recognizes our relationships.

"Do you think homosexuals are revolting? You bet your sweet ass we are!"
—LEAFLET INVITING PEOPLE TO THE FOUNDING MEETING OF THE GAY LIBERATION FRONT IN NEW YORK CITY, 1969

Gays and lesbians don't want special rights; we want equal rights. Do you believe as an American citizen you have a right to . . .

- **adopt children?**
- **raise children?**
- **marry?**
- **make love in the privacy of your home?**
- **have a romantic meal in a restaurant with your partner?**
- **have domestic partner benefits at work?**
- **have a job?**
- **work with children?**
- **buy a house?**
- **get a bank loan?**

If the radical right gets its way with its so-called family-values agenda, gays will be robbed of their basic civil liberties as guaranteed by the Fourth, Fifth, Ninth, and Fourteenth Amendments of the Constitution.

"Gays don't have legal rights. The only thing a queer couple can adopt is a highway."
—LESBIAN COMIC MAGGIE CASSELLA

As of the writing of this book, according to the ACLU . . .

- **Sexual orientation, although unrelated to an individual's ability, is still a deciding factor in employment decisions in both the public and private sectors.**

- State and local ordinances aimed at blocking equal rights for gay people are proliferating nationwide.

- A homophobic backlash has sparked a dramatic rise in hate crimes against gay people or those perceived to be gay. For example, there has been a 127 percent rise in gay murders in five major cities that kept antigay violence records between 1988 and 1993.

- Millions of Americans are still denied equality, including custody of their children and access to housing and public accommodations, because they are openly lesbian or gay, or are so perceived.

- Gay organizations on college campuses are denied official recognition, along with access to funding and campus services.

- The federal government continues its tradition of sanctioning antigay bigotry, which led, in the late 1940s and early 1950s (the McCarthy era), to the firing of at least seventeen hundred federal workers who were suspected of being lesbian or gay and were branded "perverts" and "subversives." Today, the government maintains discriminatory policies in the military and in access to security clearances, among other areas.

- Well-organized and well-funded radical right-wingers and religious fundamentalists have pledged that "gay rights will be the abortion issue of the 1990s"—meaning that the gay community's every advance toward equality will be challenged. Now that communism has more or less been neutralized as a cause to fear and hate, homosexuality has become the "curse" that faces these religious but decidedly uncharitable and unforgiving zealots. More significant, it has become the cause for their fund-raising efforts. To make these people contribute great amounts of money, they must hate something. Tag, we're it!

It's war!

The radical right has been spreading its propaganda, scaring people with "the gay agenda." You've heard it. They proclaim that gay people have an agenda to take over the country and convert children. It seems to me that

It's FRUSTRATING BEING AN ACTIVIST. I HAVE DREAMS OF TYING CLARENCE THOMAS DOWN AND SHAVING HIS LEGS WITH AN EPILADY.

Artist: Ann Glover © Judy Carter

the right-wing bigots are the ones with a gay agenda, and it is being presented in the congress of the United States of America.

"Jesse Helms and Newt Gingrich were shaking hands congratulating themselves on the introduction of an antigay bill in Congress. If it passes, they won't be able to shake hands, because it will then be illegal for a prick to touch an asshole!"
—JUDY CARTER

THE FIGHT AHEAD

"Lead—follow—or get out of the way!"
—ANONYMOUS

As we have become empowered, antigay hostility has become more open and virulent. While the radical right are genuinely homophobic, they are also targeting us because they think they can build their constituency and power base in the process. Scaring people with homophobic rhetoric, precinct by precinct, the right wing has built up a powerful base. The radical right has networks of radio stations, television shows, and churches to coordinate the distribution of its message of hate to the world and to collect money in its name. Everyone in the gay community must fight back.

Actually, we can use their attacks as an opportunity to build our own base and forward our own agendas. Committing ourselves to a positive message of freedom, we build coalitions of gays and straights. Building a base of support is one of our chief processes, as well as a chief payoff for us if we can turn crisis into opportunity. Coalitions help extend our network of friends and allies, and empower our own people in a time of danger by showing us that we are not alone. Let's get busy.

"The radical right is so homophobic that they think global warming is caused by the AIDS quilt."
—COMIC DENNIS MILLER

HERE'S WHAT YOU CAN DO

Use Your Purchasing Power by Supporting Gay-Friendly Companies

How many out gays are on the board of your mutual fund? Does the company that makes your favorite ice cream have domestic partnership benefits? If it's

Ben & Jerry's, it does. If it's Simon & Schuster, the publisher of this book, it does. You might be surprised to find out just how much of your money is going to support causes dedicated to taking away your rights. You might think you're just having a burger when you eat at Carl's Jr, but in actuality you are fueling a right-wing war chest.

The one area in which we have any clout is economics. Before giving your money away, do research and make sure your money is going to support companies who support us. And write letters to let them know that you support their progressive policies. There is an entire book out that lists all gay-friendly companies. Look in the Appendix. Get a copy. Follow it. Hopefully, you will come to the realization that changing your fast-food haunts is a small price to pay for changing the world.

Boycott

Another way to use our economic clout is to boycott any company, organization, or even state that doesn't support gay rights. In November 1992, Colorado voters enacted a state constitutional amendment—called Amendment 2—repealing all existing gay rights laws and barring any future enactment of such laws. However, when those in support of gay rights boycotted the state, the crunch was felt and the law was shot down. Not giving up, antigay activists took the matter to the Supreme Court, where once again the gay activists won. If Colorado doesn't support my rights, I don't ski on their mountains. We're here, we're queer, and we ski!

Give Your Time and Talent to Gay Organizations

Whatever your skills are, they are needed. Can you design leaflets, lick stamps, make calls, give speeches, write ad copy, use a computer, print out labels, or staple? Then get involved by donating your time. It's also a way to get out of self-absorbing. Do some good in the world and meet people.

Donate Money

If you can't give your time, give your money to gay and lesbian or-

"I did the first twenty marches in heels . . . this year I'm going for comfort."

ganizations. There are hundreds of them fighting to eradicate homophobia in everything from the legal system to schools to churches to the ski slopes. Look in the back of this book and find an organization you would like to support.

Show Up and March

Showing up means a lot. When a million gays and supporters of gays showed up for the '94 March on Washington, it was powerful. Just the act of Irish gays marching in Chicago's Saint Patrick's Day parade brought the issue to the Supreme Court.

"The police always underestimate how many gays are marching. If a cop had a ménage à trois, he would say that there were only two people there."
—JUDY CARTER

Get Active in Political Campaigns

Support gay-friendly candidates or run for office yourself. In a time when the Republicans swept congress, Sheila Kuehl, an open lesbian (she was Zelda on the *Dobie Gillis* show), won a seat in my state district in California. Don't let them scare us back into hiding. We can win.

"I'm gay, and as an elected city councilman I'm cost-effective. If I ever run for president, I can be my own first lady."
—SAN FRANCISCO CITY COUNCILMAN AND COMIC TOM AMMIANO

Start a Support Group at Work

Adopt, implement, and publicize a nondiscrimination policy relating to gays and lesbians at work. If you would like information on how to start a gay and lesbian support group at work, contact Out at Work (Or Not), 312-794-5218, or one of the many organizations listed in the Appendix.

Canvass

Walking your neighborhood for an election and outing yourself door-to-door is the most direct way to reach voters. According to Leah Campbell in the Fight the Right Action Kit, "The human interaction of the door-to-door contact breaks down false perceptions based on ignorance and the misleading messages of our opposition. The canvass is the highest quality contact a campaign can have with voters, and is most effective in swinging undecided voters in our favor."

Fund-Raise

Fund-raising can be fun, and a party is a great way to fight the right and meet people! Not only will partygoers be bringing their checkbooks; they will bring their ideas, energy, and cute friends to empower your project.

Engage in Civil Disobedience

Groups such as ACT UP and Lesbian Avengers take very direct, dramatic action in targeting companies and businesses that discriminate against gays. A lot of people with AIDS can't afford the time it takes for the system to produce results the legal way. Sometimes just a few people sitting down and stopping day-to-day business gets more results than a big march.

Speak at Public Institutions

Educating others is another way to eradicate homophobia. Volunteer to speak at schools, at work, at churches and other institutions. Or you can even organize your own speakers' bureau.

Lobby

Give money to political action committees (PACs) or lobby yourself by phoning, writing, or E-mailing your representative. It's important for them to know that people in their district are gay and that they vote too!

Wear Gay-Friendly Buttons or Pins

Since a significant part of the antigay agenda is "Don't ask, don't tell," wearing a button that identifies you as gay or gay friendly is an effective means of

protest—especially if you wear it to a meeting of the Christian Coalition!

Write Letters

Write "Support gay rights" letters. Whether to a friend, an organization, or the government, letter writing is a strong way to organize and communicate your thoughts to others. You can also organize letter-writing campaigns to influence politicians. You can even get preprinted postcards: "I support gay rights and I vote." But accord-

"Instead of outing celebrities, . . . I think we should just stop dating them."

ing to NOW activist Barbara Timmer, the best way to get attention from your government representative is to handwrite your letters. "I am a voter in your district and I'm concerned about . . ."

Get Information . . . Network

Know what's going on. Join GLAAD and Lambda, and subscribe to *The Advocate.* Go to gay events and network. In isolation we are powerless. We need to connect together as a social and political movement to protect our rights.

Subscribe to Right-Wing Papers

Infiltrate the right wing by subscribing to antigay newsletters or by listening to Rush Limbaugh on the radio. Know the enemy. They are organized and working every day to take away your rights. Check out the Appendix on how to receive right-wing information via E-mail.

Bigot-Bash Right-Wing Events

When the antigay coalition is collecting signatures in your neck of the woods, be there to give people information on what exactly it is that they are signing. The most effective way to bash a bigot is through communication and letting them see that you are not a stereotype, but a human being with many of the same concerns that they have about the well-being of society. Bigot bashing has two primary objectives: preventing signatures on antigay petitions and providing a gay-positive experience to as many people as possible.

Very often the rhetoric used by the religious right to encourage people to sign their petitions succeeds by presenting us as a menace, as evil, unlawful, distasteful people whose "special rights" agenda must be stopped. By participating in bigot busting, our mere presence deflates many of those arguments. People approaching the petitioners can see some real living, breathing, walking, and talking gays and lesbians calmly explaining the impact of right-wing initiatives. (An individual who has signed a petition earlier can become an ally when confronted with the truth.)

Create an Event

Whether it is a party to create support for a candidate, a rally against an antigay proposition, or a support group of gay and lesbian writers, an event brings people together and creates energy.

"When voters vote on an antigay proposition, they often don't know how they voted because of the way they are worded. Sometimes a 'no' vote means 'yes,' and 'yes' means 'no.' Only a

man could have written this, because only a man can take a 'no' to mean a 'yes.'"

—JUDY CARTER

Set up Booths at Public Affairs

Set up gay-rights-awareness booths at public events. Bring in a gay or lesbian speaker or comic to any straight group you belong to.

Hand Out Gay-Positive Literature

Have a lot of it handy and ready; you never know when you will need it. I like leaving it in people's bathrooms. They don't know who left the leaflets there, but it's the one place where they're sure to read them.

Use the Word Gay to Get Your Way

I know that many people think that this is politically incorrect, but we can take these myths that bigots have about us and use them to our advantage. Sometimes when I feel I'm being screwed by a company, I slip in, "You're overcharging me because I'm *gay!* That's not going to bode well in the *gay community!*" It makes them real nervous. No matter how homophobic they are, they don't want to have a bunch of dykes and queers from ACT UP picketing outside their business. This is, of course, a fear tactic, and using it is not my favorite way to proceed. But as I said earlier, this is war!

Get On-Line

One way to fight the radical right is with technology. I've always had problems writing my congressperson. Writing the letter was easy, but it was always too much hassle to find a stamp and envelope and get it to the post office. E-mail is one of the easiest and fastest ways to respond to your political representative or to the media. Practically all major newspapers, TV shows, and periodicals are on-line.

Being on-line is the easiest way to keep informed of what's going on in the gay community. There are over a thousand electronic mailing lists you can get on to be in touch with the gay community. The way they work is that you E-mail them, letting them know that you want to subscribe. You then become a part of a cyberspace loop, and you will get periodic E-mail announcements from them. You can always unsubscribe if the mailings become too much to read. One of my favorite mailing lists is ACTION-ALERT, which is "designed to provide the lesbian, gay and bisexual community with a resource by which we can respond to attacks on our community that are occurring anywhere."

And finally . . .

Come Out, Come Out, Wherever You Are
Coming out each day keeps homophobia away.

When the radical right is actively trying to push us back into the closet, coming out is itself political activism. Stay visible by coming out to a new person every day. Score two points by coming out to a member of the Christian Coalition. Coming out is a never-ending process of expressing our right to be exactly who we are without any shame. *Do* ask, *do* tell!

STRETCH: Just Do It!
Make a commitment to do one political activity this week to further equal rights for gays and lesbians. Write it down here:

By (date) _____ **I commit to**

_____

Congratulations! You are now a major homo.

One Final Word . . .

Perhaps at this point in your coming-out process you have the willingness to allow anyone to think you're gay. If you have done all the Stretches and have now come out as the major homo you are, this next idea might be a shocker:

Being gay is no big deal.

In the total scope of who you are, being gay is only a small part. Actually, if you define yourself exclusively as a gay person, you are limiting yourself as a human being and excluding yourself from being a citizen of the world.

"Anyone can be gay—it's no accomplishment—but only I can be me."
—COMPOSER NED ROREM

There is a movement in this country to sequester all that is different—all that is not Christian, English speaking, rich, white, and (of course) straight. As people who have suffered the indecency of rejection because of being different, we have, hopefully, developed the capacity to empathize with others whose basic civil rights are also violated. Yet many of us, in our need to be accepted, have adopted the current narrow mind-set of passing judgment on others. In a society where success is measured in terms of wealth, power, and acceptance, so many of us play the game of putting down others in order to raise our own status. "I may be gay, but I own two homes and I have an important job, not like *those* people." By seeing others only in terms of their differences, we ghettoize, we isolate, we become part of the problem.

Activism is not just about joining groups. It's a way of thinking. It's about accepting differences in ourselves and others while simultaneously acknowledging our sameness.

In coming out, you have gone through a powerful process of self-discovery, but don't ever forget where you've come from. Even if you have come to a place of utter self-acceptance, deep in your heart that pain of rejection, shame, and humiliation will always be with you. And because of that, you have become a gift to those who still suffer, because in experiencing your own pain, you can now understand theirs. Those people will come to you. They came to you yesterday—they have always been coming to you. But perhaps until now you haven't seen them. Or perhaps you rejected them because their differences scared you. Or maybe you were too blinded by your own self-absorption to reach out to them.

And so we go through these steps again and again, coming out not as a *gay* person but as a *complete* person, who is accepting of all he or she is. Can you love yourself unconditionally right now? Even if you read this book and didn't come out to one person, can you have that be okay for now? Can you love yourself even when it seems that the world is rejecting you? And can you love others who are also imperfect? Even having all the world accept us will not eradicate self-hate. No matter how many antidiscriminatory laws are passed or sexual orientation suits are won, it will never eradicate self-hate. And so, at the end of the coming-out process, we are back at the beginning, taking a look in the mirror and loving that person looking back at us. And hopefully the day will come when it is not necessary to come out as gay—when we can come out as just another loving human being.

To paraphrase the immortal words of good witch Glinda:

COME OUT, COME OUT WHOEVER YOU ARE

Appendix

If you would like to receive information or a brochure about Judy Carter's comedy concerts, Coming Out workshops, or just drop her a note, contact:

Closet Productions
2112 Walnut Ave., Suite #101
Venice, CA 90291
Voice: 310-915-0555
Fax: 310-398-8046
E-mail: homobooks@aol.com
Web Site: http://users.aol.com/
  homobooks

NATIONAL GAY AND LESBIAN ORGANIZATIONS

ACT UP/Golden Gate
519 Castro St., #93
San Francisco, CA 94114
Voice: 415-252-9200
Fax: 415-252-9277
Web Site: www.creative.net/~actupgg/

American Civil Liberties Union
132 West 43rd St.
New York, NY 10036
Voice: 212-944-9800
Fax: 212-869-9061

Digital Queers
584 Castro St., Suite 150
San Francisco, CA 94114
Voice: 415-252-6282
Fax: 415-252-6290
E-mail: digiqueers@aol.com

GLAAD (Gay and Lesbian Alliance
  Against Defamation)
8455 Beverly Blvd., #305
Los Angeles, CA 90048
Monitor Response Hotline: 213-
  874-5223
Voice: 213-658-6775
Fax: 213-658-6776
E-mail: GLAAD@GLAAD.ORG
NY Voice: 212-807-1700

Hollywood Supports
8455 Beverly Blvd., Suite 305
Los Angeles, CA 90048
Voice: 213-655-7705
Fax: 213-655-0955
Advocates for domestic partnership
  benefits, mainly in the entertainment
  industry.

Human Rights Campaign
1101 14th Street NW

Washington, DC 20005
Voice: 202-628-4160
Fax: 202-347-5323
E-mail: communications@hrcusa_org

Lambda—Legal Defense and Education
 Fund
666 Broadway
New York, NY 10012
Voice: 212-995-8585
Fax: 212-995-2306

NGLTF (National Gay and Lesbian Task
 Force)
2320 17th Street NW
Washington, DC 20009-2702
Voice: 202-332-6483
Fax: 202-332-0207
E-mail: ngltf@aol.com

National Organization for Women
1000 16th St. NW, Suite 700
Washington, DC 20036
Voice: 202-331-0066

Out at Work (Or Not)
Jason Cohen
P.O. Box 359
Chicago, IL 60690-0359
Voice: 312-794-5218
E-mail: oawon@aol.com

People For the American Way
2000 M Street, NW, Suite 400
Washington, DC 20036

BOOKS

Breaking the Surface, Greg Louganis,
 Plume Books, 1996
*The Corporate Closet: The Professional
 Lives of Gay Men in America*, James D.
 Woods and Jay Lucas, Free Press,
 1993
*Cracking the Corporate Closet: The 200
 Best (and Worst) Companies to Work
 For, Buy From, and Invest In if You're*
*Gay or Lesbian—and Even if You're
 Not*, Daniel Baker, Sean Strub and Bill
 Henning, HarperCollins, 1995
Gay Yellow Pages, Renaissance House,
 1995, Voice: 212-674-0120
The Guide to Living with HIV Infection,
 John Bartlett and Ann K. Finkbeiner,
 The Johns Hopkins University Press,
 1991
Growing Up Gay, Funny Gay Males, Hy-
 perion, 1994
Is It a Choice?, Eric Marcus, Harper-
 Collins, 1993
*Finding True Love in a Man-Eat-Man
 World*, Craig Nelson, Dell Trade Pa-
 perbook, 1996
Heather Has Two Mommies, Leslea New-
 man and Alyson Wonderland, Alyson
 Publishing, 1989
Lesbian Sex, JoAnn Loulan, Spinsters
 Ink, 1984
The New Joy of Gay Sex, Dr. Charles Sil-
 verstein and Felice Picano, Harper
 Perennial, 1992
Now That You Know, Betty Fairchild and
 Nancy Hayward, Harvest Books, 1989
*Reinventing the Family: Lesbian and Gay
 Parents*, Laura Benkov, Ph.D, Random
 House, 1994 paperback
*Stranger at the Gate: To Be Gay and
 Christian in America*, Mel White,
 Plume Books, 1995
*Virtual Equality—The Mainstreaming of
 Gay and Lesbian Liberation*, Urvashi
 Vaid, Anchor Books, 1995
What the Bible Really Says, David
 Helminiak, Alamo Square Press, 1994
Who Cares If It's a Choice? Ellen Orlean,
 Laugh Line Press, 1994

MAGAZINES

The Advocate
800-827-0561

Bad Attitude
SM lesbians
P.O. Box 390110
Cambridge, MA 02139

Curve
2336 Market St., #15
San Francisco, CA 94114
818-760-8983

Genre
7080 Hollywood Blvd., #1104
Hollywood, CA 90028
213-896-9778

Girl Friends
800-475-3763

Out
110 Greene St., #6000
New York, NY 10012
E-mail: outmag@aol.com

Poz
Hope, Health, HIV
Realtime Inc.
800-973-2376

HOTLINES

Note: This is a partial list. If you need any further referrals to gay and lesbian services in your area, contact NGLTF at 202-332-6483.

ALABAMA

Gay/Lesbian Information Line,
Lambda, Inc.
P.O. Box 55913
Birmingham, 35255
205-326-8600

ALASKA

Gay Helpline
Identity, Inc.

P.O. Box 200070
Anchorage, 99520
907-258-4777

ARIZONA

Lesbian/Gay Community Switchboard
P.O. Box 16423
Phoenix, 85011
602-234-2752

ARKANSAS

Arkansas Gay & Lesbian Task Force
  Switchboard
P.O. Box 45053
Little Rock, 72214
501-666-3340 (Little Rock)
800-448-8305 (Statewide)

CALIFORNIA

Gay & Lesbian Community Services
  Center
1213 N. Highland Ave.
Los Angeles, 90038
213-464-7400 (Switchboard)
213-464-0029 (TDD)
213-464-1702 (Fax)

COLORADO

Drawer E,
1245 E. Colfax, #125
Denver, 80218
303-831-6268
303-837-1598 (Helpline)

CONNECTICUT

Gay, Lesbian & Bisexual Community
  Center
1841 Broad St.
Hartford, 06114-1780
203-724-5524

DELAWARE

Gay & Lesbian Alliance of Delaware
800 West St.
Wilmington, 19801-1526
302-655-5280
800-292-0429 (Hotline)

DISTRICT OF COLUMBIA

Gay & Lesbian Hotline
Whitman-Walker Clinic
1407 S St. NW
Washington, DC, 20009
202-833-3234
202-332-2192 (Spanish Line)

FLORIDA

Gay & Lesbian Community Hotline of
    Greater Miami
c/o Lambda Passages
7545 Biscayne Blvd.
Miami, 33138
305-759-3661

Gay/Lesbian Community Services of
    Central Florida
P.O. Box 533446/750 W Colonial Drive
Orlando, 32853-3446
407-843-4297 (Hotline)
407-649-8615 (Office)

GEORGIA

Atlanta Gay Center
63 12th St.
Atlanta, 30309
404-876-5372 (Helpline)
404-892-0661 (TDD)

HAWAII

Gay Information Service
P.O. Box 37083
Honolulu, 96837-0083
808-926-1000

IDAHO

The Community Center (TCC)
P.O. Box 323
Boise, 83701
208-336-3870

ILLINOIS

Lesbian & Gay Helpline
Horizons Community Services
961 W. Montana
Chicago, 60614
312-472-6469 (Helplines)
312-929-HELP
312-327-HELP (TDD)

INDIANA

Gay/Lesbian Switchboard/Community
    Referral Service
P.O. Box 2152
Indianapolis, 46206
317-253-GAYS

IOWA

Gay & Lesbian Resource Center
4211 Grand Ave.
Des Moines, 50312
515-279-2110
515-277-1454 (Information Line)

KANSAS

Wichita Gay Info Line
P.O. Box 16782
Wichita, 67216-0782
316-269-0913

KENTUCKY

Gay & Lesbian Hotline
P.O. Box 2796
Louisville, 40201
502-454-6699

LOUISIANA

St. Louis Community Center
1022 Barracks St.
New Orleans, 70116
504-524-7023

MAINE

Gay/Lesbian Phoneline
c/o P.O. Box 990
Caribou, 04736
207-498-2088

MARYLAND

Gay & Lesbian Community Center
241 W. Chase St.
Baltimore, 21201
410-837-5445
410-837-8888 (Switchboard)
410-837-8529 (TDD)
410-837-8512 (Fax)

MASSACHUSETTS

Boston Gay & Lesbian Helpline
617-267-9001 (Voice & TTY)

MICHIGAN

Lesbian & Gay Community Network of
    Western Michigan
909 Cherry St. SE
Grand Rapids, 49506-1403
616-241-GAYS (Switchboard)

MINNESOTA

Gay & Lesbian Community Action
    Council
Minneapolis/St. Paul
612-822-8661 (Hotline)

MISSISSIPPI

Mississippi Gay & Lesbian Alliance
P.O. Box 8342
Jackson, 39284-8342
601-353-7611 (Switchboard)
800-537-0851 (MS only)

MISSOURI

Gay Services Network
Gay Talk Helpline
P.O. Box 32592
Kansas City, 64111
816-931-4470

MONTANA

Montana Lesbian Coalition
Mail to: MLC, P.O. Box 1283
Helena, 59624

NEBRASKA

A.N.G.L.E., Inc.
P.O. Box 31375
Omaha, 68131-0375
402-339-9948

NEVADA

Gay Switchboard
c/o Metropolitan Community Church
1119 S. Main St.
Las Vegas, 89104-1026
702-733-9990

NEW HAMPSHIRE

Gay Info Line of New Hampshire
P.O. Box 3148
Nashua, 03061-3148
603-595-2650

NEW JERSEY

Gay Activists of New Jersey
P.O. Box 1734
South Hackensack, 07606
201-692-1794 (Helpline)

NEW MEXICO

Common Bond, Inc.
P.O. Box 26836
Albuquerque, 87125
505-266-8041 (Information/Helpline)

NEW YORK

Lesbian & Gay Community Services
   Center
208 W. 13th St.
New York, 10011
212-620-7310

Gay & Lesbian Switchboard of New York
212-777-1800

Lesbian Switchboard, New York
212-741-2610

NORTH CAROLINA

Alternative Resources of the Triad
P.O. Box 4442
Greensboro, 27404
919-275-1834
919-274-2100 (Hotline)

NORTH DAKOTA

Prairie Lesbian & Gay Community
P.O. Box 83
Moorhead, MN 56560
701-237-0556 (North Dakota & Western
   Minnesota)

OHIO

Gay & Lesbian Community Switchboard
P.O. Box 9480
Cincinnati, 45209
513-221-7800

Lesbian & Gay Community Center of
   Greater Cleveland
P.O. Box 6177/1418 W. 29th
Cleveland, 44101
216-522-1999
216-781-6736 (Hotline)

OKLAHOMA

TOHR Gay/Lesbian Helpline
P.O. Box 52729
Tulsa, 74152-2729
918-743-GAYS

OREGON

Gay & Lesbian Community Center
P.O. Box 813/3856 Carnes Rd.
Roseburg, 97470-0166
503-679-9144
503-672-4126 (Switchboard)

PENNSYLVANIA

Philadelphia Lesbian & Gay Task Force
1501 Cherry St.
Philadelphia, 19102
215-563-9584
215-563-4581 (Hotline)

PUERTO RICO

Amigas y Amigos de los Derechos
   Humanos
106 Ave de Diego
Box 242
Santurce, 00907

RHODE ISLAND

Gay/Lesbian Helpline of Rhode Island
P.O. Box 5671
Providence, 02903
401-751-3322

SOUTH CAROLINA

Gay & Lesbian Switchboard
c/o Palmetto Gay/Lesbian Association
P.O. Box 10022 Federal Stn
Greenville, 29603-0022
803-271-4207

SOUTH DAKOTA

The Coalition
P.O. Box 89803
Sioux Falls, 57105
605-332-4599

TENNESSEE

Tennessee Gay & Lesbian Alliance
  (TGALA)
P.O. Box 41305
Nashville, 37204-1305
615-292-4820

TEXAS

Gay & Lesbian Switchboard of Houston
P.O. Box 66469
Houston, 77266-6469
713-529-3211

UTAH

Gay/Lesbian Alliance of Cache Valley
  (GLA-CV)
UMC 0100, Box 119
Tagart Student Center
Logan, 84322-0100
801-752-1129

VERMONT

Vermont Coalition of Lesbians & Gay Men
P.O. Box 1125
Montpelier, 05602

VIRGINIA

Gay Information Line
P.O. Box 1325
Norfolk, 23501
804-622-GAYS
804-623-BARS

WASHINGTON

Lesbian/Gay Resource Center
CAB 305
Evergreen State College
Olympia, 98505
206-866-6000, ext. 6544

WEST VIRGINIA

Gay & Lesbian Helpline
c/o Mountaineers
Student Organization Wing
Mountainlair, WVU
Morgantown, 26506
304-292-GAY2

WISCONSIN

Gay/Lesbian Phone Line
P.O. Box 310
Madison, 53701
608-255-4297
608-255-0743 (Women)

WYOMING

United Gays & Lesbians of Wyoming
P.O. Box 2037
Laramie, 82070
307-635-4301

WORLDWIDE WEB RESOURCES

Political, lesbian & gay, news and reference, and more.
(Cruised and edited by Karen Wickre, co-founder of Digital Queers.)

GAY, QUEER, AND RELATED

Homo Handbook Web Site

http://members.aol.com/homobooks
Fabulous! Fabulous! Fabulous! Coming out becomes high tech as you hear and watch some of the best gay and lesbian humor; participate in the Coming Out Forum; hot link to other gay and lesbian sites and chat with Judy.

Yahoo Internet Guide

http://www.yahoo.com/society_and_
    culture/gays_lesbians_and_bisexuals/
Yahoo can link you to everything you want to know about gays, lesbians, bis, transgenders, hot chatting, organizations and spandex.

Gay and Lesbian Forum on America On-line

Includes multi-interest bulletin boards, library files, Lambda bookstores, events, politics and gay and lesbian "heart-to-heart" personals.

http://coos.dartmouth.edu/~jcollins/ kataBisex.html

Essays, links to more queer and bi info, including a long bisexual resource list, updated monthly.

Digital Queers

http://www.dq.org/dq/
They're here, they're queer, they have a Web page (in the making).

Gay, Lesbian and Straight Teachers Network (GLSTN)

http://www.glstn.org/freedom/
Lots of resources here for the interested teacher or student—tools with which to battle homophobia in and out of the classroom. GLSTN is a young organization that is quickly becoming known around the country as a place to turn.

Hollywood Supports

http://www.datalounge.com/hsupports
HS offers diversity training and lots of information about companies offering domestic partner benefits, lesbian and gay employee groups, and so on. There are currently 250 companies listed here—and HS keeps the list up to date.

Human Rights Campaign

http://www.hrcusa.org/
This new page with the new name (the group is dropping "Fund"), includes a "one-stop activism center" through which you can get the lowdown on your congresspersons, and easy E-mail/fax contact with them on issues of interest.

Infoqueer

http://www.infoqueer.org/queer/qis/
Great meta-view—cleanly organized topical pages (arts and culture, organizations, publications, etc.), with links to women's sites, HIV and AIDS info, and home pages of people who are *out* on the Web! Thanks to David Stazer and the Berkeley Queer Info Center for putting this together.

L.A. Gay and Lesbian Community Services Center

http://www.glcsc.org
A model for other community centers around the country from one of the largest. L.A.-based events and meetings, and also community resources, are featured.

Lesbian.Org

http://www.lesbian.org/
Ms. Amy Goodloe, aka The List Mistress, has created a meta-page of resources for lesbians and feminists. Very useful.

National Gay and Lesbian Task Force
http://www.ngltf.org
The grande dame of GLBT organizations (in this lifetime, anyway) offers a taste of their prodigious white papers and reports on topics ranging from hate crime to gay marriage.

Out.Com
http://www.out.com/
Out magazine on-line, with references and links to current and past issue material, local resource and event listings, and more.

!OutProud!
http://www.outproud.org/outproud/
This is the home of a helpful searchable database of use to teens and young people looking for information about groups where they live. Just enter an area code or zip code to get local listings of support groups, activist groups, and more.

PlanetOut!
http://www.planetout.com/
This is the enterprise created by DQ cofounder Tom Rielly, which will launch an extensive LGTB information/entertainment/social Web site. Send E-mail for info to info@planetout.com.

Queer Resources Directory
http://www.qrd.org/qrd/
The parent of all queer (lesbian, gay, bisexual, transgender) information on the Net. Created by Dr. Ron Buckmire (Occidental College), maintained by David Casti, Net-maven supreme. This is a large unregulated library of topics, newsletters, publications, archives, contact info, and more, on families, religion, youth, HIV and AIDS resources, media, culture and history, politics and activism, a directory of organizations, business and legal issues. A great place to begin.

YouthArts Project
http://spidey.usc.edu/qf/yap/index.html
This is a collaborative effort between writer Patricia Nell Warren and an L.A.-based gay youth group sponsored by USC. Links to other resources for gay and lesbian kids.

HIV and SEXUAL HEALTH INFO

AIDS Info Database by Ben Gardiner
http://itsa.ucsf.edu/~beng/aidsbbs.html
Ben's very helpful digest of published articles is here, along with PWA messages on treatments, and not one but two glossaries of terms. Send E-mail to Ben at beng@itsa.ucsf.edu.

AIDS Treatment News
http://gopher.hivnet.org:70/ls/
magazines/atn
Searchable database—every issue (now biweekly). John James's yeomanlike production is filed here, from its beginning in April 1986 through the latest biweekly issue. You can also reach ATN by E-mail at aidsnews@aidsnews.org, or by calling 800-TREAT-1-2.

ARIC's Index of On-line AIDS Info Resources
http://www.critpath.org/aric/pwarg-8.htm
ARIC is the AIDS Research Information Center in Baltimore. They offer a huge annotated list of sites, including newsgroups, government files, many scientific and medical publications. There are also links to international news, academic, professional and activist/advocacy resources.

Marty Howard's HIV/AIDS Home Page
http://www.smartlink.net/~martinjh/
Marty's home page is a labor of love, full of annotated links and services, e.g., participation in a weekly survey posted by doctors or grad students wanting info from the AIDS community; clinical trial and

medication information; lots of pointers to relevant newsgroups. He also offers a very easy way to subscribe to mailing and announcement lists for everything from support groups to the influential sci.med.aids newsgroup to the CDC AIDS daily newsletter, and also *AIDS Treatment News, GAYPOZ, GMHC Issues,* the *AIDS Information Newsletter,* and Caregivers Support Group.

Project Inform
http://www.projinf.org/
Here are discussion papers and fact sheets on treatment strategies, "Doctor, Patient and HIV," and Antivirals A to Z.

SUMERIA The Immune System
http://www.livelinks.com/sumeria/
A helpful PWA named Justin J. has put together a very nice page of book reviews, articles, interviews, and a couple of personal essays that are quite wonderful. Don't miss "Be as Wise as the Serpents You Encounter" at <http://www.livelinks. com/sumeria/aids/justin.html> and his annotated reading list of recommended books and newsgroups.

UC Berkeley Gopher Files on AIDS
gopher://uclink.berkeley.edu:1901/11/ other/aids
This large site contains text-only files on many HIV services, education and advocacy, as well as links to Positive Planet, safe-sex toys, and more.

Coalition for Positive Sexuality: Sex Ed for Your Head
http://www.positive.org/cps/index.html
This is a totally excellent place for teens and enlightened others—women, men, bi, straight and gay—to get factual, no-BS info in English or Spanish. Learn about consent laws, order useful books. There's a terrific resources page on AIDS, services for runaways, women's health, STDs

and tests, activism, and all kinds of hotlines. Great graphics and a great feeling from a Chicago group.

The Safer Sex Page
http://www.safersex.org/
John Troyer's award-winning page has lots of Q&A about condoms, research on safer sex methods, information geared to counselors and women, and a forum for your comments, called Shout Out!

He includes good links to safe-sex vendors like Condom Country <www.ag.com/ condom/country>, Good Vibrations <www. goodvibes.com>, Blowfish <www.blowfish. com> and Condomania <http://www.condomania.com/>

TRANSGENDER INFO

Kate Bornstein: A Transgender Transsexual Postmodern Tiresias
http://english.hss.cmu.edu/ctheory/a-kate_bornstein.html
Excerpts from *Gender Outlaw* and Kate's play, *The Opposite Is Neither!,* and including an interview with feminist theorist Shannon Bell.

The Transgender Forum
http://www.zoom.com/personal/cindym/ indextg.html
Here is informative, funny, and well-organized information about everything from transvestites to transsexuals and in between. Links to organizations, catalogs and shopping info, libraries geared to ftm and mtf interests. Look for RuPaul and other TV stars.

WOMEN'S RESOURCES

Feminist Activist Resources on the Net
http://www.igc.apc.org/women/feminist. html
This index page has links to news, re-

sources for political activism, and issues pages: women of color, domestic violence, health, reproductive rights, global subject areas. Sarah Stapleton-Gray created the page, and we thank her.

Women's Wire Home Page
http://www.women.com/
Politics, business, news, features from a '90s feminist perspective.

PROGRESSIVE, LIBERAL, AND RELATED

American Civil Liberties Union
http://www.aclu.org
What would we do without them? Follow the hijinks and low blows in the effort to overcome the threats to our civil rights.

The Electronic Activist
http://www.crocker.com/~ifas/activist/
Statewide directory of contact info for legislators, TV and radio stations, and more. Includes guidelines for effective communication about your issues. From the Institute for First Amendment Studies.

The Freedom Forum
http://www.nando.net/prof/freedom/1994/freedom.html
On-line magazine and media studies topics explored regularly include gay issues, the info highway, diversity and race, politics and the media, and more. Excellent think pieces, speeches, papers and discussion topics.

Internet Civil Liberty Resources
http://www.intac.com/~kgs/freedom/kadie.html
Carl Kadie, avid librarian/civil libertarian, has created links to various freedom of expression/civil liberties resources on the Web. Includes newsgroups and mailing lists.

Liberty Library: A Home Page
ttp://falcon.cc.ukans.edu/~cubsfan/liberal.html
Libertarian readings and links, both to official Libertarian Party info and to informal documents. Created out of the Liberty Conference on The WELL.

NewtWatch Home Page
http://www.cais.com/newtwatch/
Amusing page of Newt-tweaks, i.e., the five ethics committee cases pending against him, a bird's-eye view of Newt's office expenses and staff salaries, and more.

Turn Left: The Home of Liberalism
http://falcon.cc.ukans.edu/~cubsfan/liberal.html
A very complete page of liberal resources on the Net, including "resources dedicated to fighting conservatism," worldwide liberalism info, foreign policy, economic and social issue links. Mike Silverman put it together.

CONSERVATIVE—AND WORSE

The Christian Broadcasting Network
http://the700club.org/
Pat Robertson's home stomping grounds. Includes the monthly 700 Club viewer guide and where to find it in your area. If you haven't already, do tune in. Don't miss CBN's Hotlist: "A guide to Good on the Web."

Christian Coalition
http://cc.org/
This extensive page even features audio clips of Dick Armey, Bob Dole, Newt, and others extolling the CC viewpoint. There's a "scorecard" area to track legislative support, plus press releases, voters' guides and opinion polls, and how to contact congressfolk.

The Family Research Council
http://www.frc.org/
An avid pro-nuclear-family group based in Washington. Its mission: "to reaffirm and promote nationally . . . the traditional family unit and the Judeo-Christian value system upon which it is built." Here are the council's stands on issues, how to subscribe for regular info, etc.

GOPAC
http://www.gopac.com/
Newt Gingrich's PAC, which encourages conservatives to be trained and to run for political jobs at every level. This page links to audio tapes, training seminars, regional conferences, citizen activist kits, and more.

The Progress and Freedom Foundation
http://www.townhall.com/pff
This is the nonprofit incarnation of GOPAC.

Focus on the Family
http://www.cs.albany.edu/~ault/fof/fofbegin.html
The ultraconservative Christian organization in Colorado Springs has an unofficial page, with its newsletters, various alerts, information on the FOF radio program, E-mail and FTP sites.

The Grand Old Page
http://www.berkeleyic.com/gop
The GOP (get it?) features a direct-fax-to-Limbaugh feature you can access for *free*; don't forget to edit the subject line to describe the issue you're writing about (and also the return E-mail address, in case you want to leave it blank or specify a different return E-mail address than the one you're using to send the fax).

The Right Side of the Web
http://www.clark.net/pub/jeffd/index.html

Includes "The Speaker's Corner," a Newt fan page, Rush Limbaugh info page and audio clips, hot link to conservative college groups and publications, and links to conservative pages by topic, e.g., economics, foreign policy, and "The Right Side BBS." Great overview of Those Who Wish Us Harm.

Stormfront: White Nationalists Page
http://stormfront.wat.com/stormfront/
Commentary and letters from readers on topics including Waco, Ruby Ridge, Oklahoma City, and "racial realities." Also a White Nationalism FAQ. Links to BBSs and newsgroups of the same type. Note: Also available in German and Spanish.

POLITICS AND GOVERNMENT

E-Mail Democracy
http://www.primenet.com/solutions/congress/democracy.htm
Why waste paper, time, and money? Click on the hot link for your senators and congressional reps and head directly to their E-mail addresses. Send them a message or two, and you can post same to this site for others to read. A form lets you compose and mail your message from the page.

Fedworld Home Page
http://www.fedworld.gov/
A handy compilation of U.S. government info servers by subject category; National Technical Information Service (technical, scientific, business titles and software from the feds); government reports. Also links to FTP and TELNET sites for the government (documents and files), freebie catalogs, and more.

Government Printing Office
http://thorplus.lib.purdue.edu/gpo/
This is a project of the library school of Purdue University. A rich page leads you

to WAIS databases of current bills in Congress, an index of the *Congressional Record,* the most recent two years of the *Federal Register,* text of bills up for consideration over the past two years, a link to the most recent public laws, and the U.S. Code.

Political Information Home Page
http://pages.prodigy.com/ks/lawyer/gov.html

This page starts with the basics: links to the U.S. Constitution and Declaration of Independence, the White House Home Page, and several Cabinet and Supreme Court pages. There are links to all of the presidential libraries, Republican and Democratic points of interest, and E-mail links to both Clinton and Gore.

Political Site of the Day!
http://ross.clendon.com/siteoftheday.html

This clever page selects one site, Monday through Friday, that is "entertaining, informative and/or relevant to the current political discourse." Ideology doesn't count.

State and Local Governments
http://www.loc.gov/global/state/stategov.html

Here are meta-indexes to individual state Internet resources, Web pages of cities and states, state government information via several searchers and the Council of State Governments. Link to state maps, too.

THOMAS: Legislative Information on the Internet
http://thomas.loc.gov/

Named for Thomas Jefferson, this server features the full text of bills brought before the current and the just-ended Congress; *Congressional Record* and index to same for two Congresses. Even better, there are links to "hot bills" by topic,

short name, number, which have become law, which are up for consideration this week. There are links to gopher files of Senate FAQs, directories of House members, E-mail addresses for selected House and Senate members and their committees. Don't miss the congressional audit results if you need ammo when facing the IRS! And the poll-watcher's favorite, C-SPAN, can be reached via gopher or Web link.

JUST FOR FUN

Mr. Showbiz
http://www.starwave.com/mrshowbiz.html

One of the best commercial sites covering TV, movies, concerts, all the pop culture you could wish for.

QX Magazine
London-based gay mag with rude nudity thrown in. Articles, personals, reviews. Check out the scene where Big Ben lives.
http://www.dircon.co.uk/qxmag/

And some hot cyber spots:
http://www.hotmen.com/hotspots.htmhot spots.htm
http://www.gayweb.com/
http://www.gaycafe.com/index.html

GAY AND LESBIAN E-MAIL MAILING LISTS

A great way to stay in touch is signing up for gay-related E-mail announcements. It's free, and if you would like to find out about any of the lists mentioned below, they are available in the Queer Resources Directory on the Internet at vector.casti.com by gopher, FTP or E-mail.

abbs: AIDS BBS mailing list

action-alert: Action Alert distribution list (Fight the Right!)

act-up: ACT UP mailing list

alternates: "Alternate Lifestyles" mailing list

arenal: LGB Spanish-language mailing list

bears: Bears mailing list

biact-1: Bisexual Activists list

bifem-1: Bisexual Womyn and Feminists mailing list

bisexu-1: Bisexual Discussion list

bithry-1: Bisexual Theory list

cd-forum: Cross-Dressing Forum

chorus: Lesbian/Gay/Bisexual Chorus mailing list

clgsg-1: Coalition of Lesbian and Gay Student Groups mailing list

dignity: Dignity (Catholic GLB) mailing list

domestic: Domestic Partnership mailing list

dont-tell: "Don't Ask, Don't Tell" mailing list

dsa-lgb: Democratic Socialists of America LGB Caucus mailing list

eagles: Gay Eagle Scouts mailing list

ftr-strategy: Fight the Right Strategy

gay-libn: Gay/Lesbian/Bisexual Librarians Network

gaybits: LGBT Discussion mailing list

gaydads: Gay/bi dads, dads-to-be, or daddy wanna-bes

gaynet: LGBT Discussion mailing list digest

gegstaff: GLB Geographers List

gl-asb: Gay and Lesbian S/M and Bondage list

gla-infosystems: Gay and Lesbian Americans Infosystems

gla-list: Gay and Lesbian Americans mailing list

gla-membership: Gay and Lesbian Americans Membership Committee

gla-mission: Gay and Lesbian Americans Mission Statement Committee

gla-steering: Gay and Lesbian Americans Steering Committee

glb-medical: GLB Medical Students mailing list

glb-news: Distribution list of news of interest to LGBTF (folk)

glbpoc: GLB People of Color mailing list

iglhrc: Int'l Gay and Lesbian Human Rights Commission mailing list

kenslist: Ken's list

khush: LGB South Asian mailing list

lis: Lesbians in Science mailing list

living: Womyn Living with a Disability (women only)

luti: Lesbigay Christians mailing list

medgay-l: Gay and Lesbian Medieval Studies mailing list

moms: Lesbian Moms mailing list (women only)

noglstp: Gay and Lesbian Scientists and Technical Professionals

outil: OUT in Linguistics mailing list

politidykes: POLITIDYKES—political, progressive! (women only)

qgv: Queer Global Village mailing list

qn: Queer Nation mailing list

queer-parents: LGB moms, dads, co-moms & co-dads, & mommy and daddy wanna-bes

queerplanet: Queer Planet mailing list

regayn: LGB Addiction Recovery mailing list

sappho: Forum and Support Group for Lesbian and Bisexual Women (women only)

sappho-digest: Lesbian and Bisexual Women digest (women only)

stonewall25: Stonewall25 (June 1994) mailing list

transgen: Transgender mailing list